Ransom

A Drama in Three Acts

by
Cyril Hume
and
Richard Maibaum

A Samuel French Acting Edition

New York Hollywood London Toronto

SAMUELFRENCH.COM

Copyright © 1954, Under title "Fearful Decision," as a television play by Cyril Hume and Richard Maibaum
Copyright © 1954, Under title "The Dave Decision," a play in three acts by Cyril Hume and Richard Maibaum
Copyright © 1963, (Revised and Rewritten) Cyril Hume and Richard Maibaum

ALL RIGHTS RESERVED

CAUTION: Professionals and amateurs are hereby warned that *RANSOM* is subject to a Licensing Fee. It is fully protected under the copyright laws of the United States of America, the British Commonwealth, including Canada, and all other countries of the Copyright Union. All rights, including professional, amateur, motion picture, recitation, lecturing, public reading, radio broadcasting, television and the rights of translation into foreign languages are strictly reserved. In its present form the play is dedicated to the reading public only.

The amateur live stage performance rights to *RANSOM* are controlled exclusively by Samuel French, Inc., and licensing arrangements and performance licenses must be secured well in advance of presentation. PLEASE NOTE that amateur Licensing Fees are set upon application in accordance with your producing circumstances. When applying for a licensing quotation and a performance license please give us the number of performances intended, dates of production, your seating capacity and admission fee. Licensing Fees are payable one week before the opening performance of the play to Samuel French, Inc., at 45 W. 25th Street, New York, NY 10010.

Licensing Fee of the required amount must be paid whether the play is presented for charity or gain and whether or not admission is charged.

Stock licensing fees quoted upon application to Samuel French, Inc.

For all other rights than those stipulated above, apply to: Samuel French, Inc.

Particular emphasis is laid on the question of amateur or professional readings, permission and terms for which must be secured in writing from Samuel French, Inc.

Copying from this book in whole or in part is strictly forbidden by law, and the right of performance is not transferable.

Whenever the play is produced the following notice must appear on all programs, printing and advertising for the play: "Produced by special arrangement with Samuel French, Inc."

Due authorship credit must be given on all programs, printing and advertising for the play.

No one shall commit or authorize any act or omission by which the copyright of, or the right to copyright, this play may be impaired.

No one shall make any changes in this play for the purpose of production.

Publication of this play does not imply availability for performance. Both amateurs and professionals considering a production are strongly advised in their own interests to apply to Samuel French, Inc., for written permission before starting rehearsals, advertising, or booking a theatre.

No part of this book may be reproduced, stored in a retrieval system, or transmitted in any form, by any means, now known or yet to be invented, including mechanical, electronic, photocopying, recording, videotaping, or otherwise, without the prior written permission of the publisher.

ISBN 978-0-573-61464-4   Printed in U.S.A.   #20008

STORY OF THE PLAY

Davie Stannard, seven years old, is kidnapped from his school by a woman impersonating his pediatrician's nurse. At their luxurious home in a fashionable suburb of a small mid-west metropolis, Davie's father, D. J. Stannard, an aggressive young tycoon who manufactures vacuum cleaners, promises his lovely wife, Edith, he will get their son back. That evening Stannard is telephoned by the bogus nurse's accomplice who demands $500,000 ransom. With his wife on the verge of collapse Stannard agrees to pay, and the money is assembled by Al, his brother and business associate. However, Stannard learns from Charlie Telfer, a veteran newspaperman and one time alcoholic, that apart from the moral issue involved in submitting to a criminal demand, cold statistics indicate the payment of ransom does not increase the chances of getting a kidnapped person back. On the contrary, if his son is still alive, the kidnapper's belief that the crime will be profitable may be the factor that causes the boy's death. Torn between love for his wife and child and his conviction that he is doing the right thing for all concerned, Stannard appears on a television program sponsored by his own company, and tells the kidnappers he will pay no ransom, not a penny. He appeals to them not to commit a profitless crime. Unless they return the boy unharmed he will offer the $500,000, all he has, as a reward for their apprehension. Except for Telfer and his middle-aged negro butler, Chapman, Stannard is universally condemned as a man more concerned with money than his son's life. Almost deranged, Edith pleads with him to change his mind. When he refuses she tries to rush out of the house to appeal to the hostile crowd outside to help her. Later the Police Chief, Horgan, brings Stannard Davie's bloodstained T-shirt found in an abandoned car. Blamed for Davie's apparent death, Stannard is ostracized and Al takes Edith out of the house at her request. While Stannard holds himself together, arranging his affairs to set up a fund to help the next American family whose child is kidnapped, Telfer, unable to bear the sight of Stannard's suffering, suicidally begins drinking again. Abandoned by everyone but Chapman, Stannard finally breaks. A few moments later Davie quietly enters, explaining to his overjoyed father that the kidnappers released him and the blood on his T-shirt got there when he bit the hand of the woman who took him from the school. Stannard's courage and wisdom have triumphed and he leads Davie out to reunite him with his mother as the crowd outside the house roars its approval.

CAST
(In the Order of Their Appearance)

> CHAPMAN
> SHIRLEY LORRAINE
> EDITH STANNARD
> D. J. STANNARD
> DAVIE STANNARD
> CHIEF HORGAN
> CHARLIE TELFER
> DR. GORMAN
> MRS. PARTRIDGE
> NURSE
> AL STANNARD
> LANGLY
> GEORGE PORTALIS
> DIGGES
> SARECKI

DRESSER, TV DIRECTOR, TV TECHNICIANS, TV CAMERAMEN, REPORTERS, NEWS PHOTOGRAPHERS, POLICEMEN, VOICES IN THE STREET.

SCENE: The entire action of the play takes place in the living room of D. J. Stannard's residence on Summit Street in an exclusive suburb of a small mid-western metropolis.

TIME: The present. September.

ACT ONE

SCENE 1: *Early morning.*
SCENE 2: *4 P.M. That afternoon.*
SCENE 3: *11 P.M. That night.*

ACT TWO

SCENE 1: *Afternoon. Two days later.*
SCENE 2: *That evening.*

ACT THREE

SCENE 1: *Next morning.*
SCENE 2: *The following morning.*

DESCRIPTION OF CHARACTERS

D. J. STANNARD: Well set-up, late thirties, graduate of a middle-western State University, an aggressive successful vacuum cleaner manufacturer, somewhat overly devoted to his business.

EDITH STANNARD: His wife, thirty-two, attractive, chic, on her toes, a good mother, very much in love with her husband, interested in civic and cultural matters.

DAVIE STANNARD: Their seven-year-old son, physically like his father, a secure, well-adjusted child.

AL STANNARD: D.J.'s brother, nominally Stannard Vacuum's General Manager. An inch or two shorter than D.J. but powerful and stocky. There is an indefinable stamp of mediocrity about him.

CHARLIE TELFER: Late forties, a veteran newspaperman and one time alcoholic, with a likably shrewd, cynical, tough face. His clothes are rumpled, his manner blunt.

CHIEF HORGAN: Rawboned, moustached, gray-haired, in his early fifties, with a slight limp. A good police officer but not above playing politics.

CHAPMAN: The Stannards' middle-aged negro butler. Although Charlie calls him an Uncle Tom, he is his own man with great natural dignity and innate understanding. Deeply religious and emotional.

SHIRLEY LORRAINE: The Stannard maid, Chapman's niece, a pretty, mettlesome girl of nineteen.

LANGLY: Comptroller of Stannard Vacuum, middle forties, with the personality of a used car salesman. Obsequious, covertly spiteful.

DR. GORMAN: The Stannard family physician, middle-aged, sympathetic, devoted to his patients, quietly effective.

MISS PARTRIDGE: Fifty, smart, slim, tweedy, with trim ankles and a still piquant profile. Carefully blue-rinsed gray hair. Elegant, confident, she is the Head Mistress of an exclusive private school.

NURSE: Capable, concerned, sympathetic R.N. in her middle forties.

DIGGES: Stannard's next door neighbor. Diffident, balding, childless, fussy, belatedly good-neighborish.

GEORGE PORTALIS: Master of Ceremonies of the Stannard Vacuum TV show. Outwardly suave and poised, but a sentimental ham at heart.

SARECKI: Tough, businesslike FBI agent. Early thirties.

Ransom

ACT ONE

Scene 1

SCENE: *The living room of the* STANNARD *residence in the glossiest suburb of a minor mid-western metropolis. Everything is pleasantly modern—materials, colors, furnishings, general arrangement and design. Off-Center, rear Left, the entrance from a large foyer is balanced by a fireplace, off-Center, rear Right. A large sofa to Left of fireplace which is flanked on the Right by bookcases opposite sofa. Tucked in behind the bookcase in rear Right corner of the room is an elegant small bar with two stools in front of it. Downstage from the bar in the Right wall are glass sliding doors looking out on a patio. Near the doors, a small table and two chairs. In the rear Left corner of the room is a spinet and bench. Downstage from them in the Left wall are two recessed windows looking out on the street. Between them stands a secretary and a chair. Downstage Left is a large wing-chair facing the audience. A TV set is positioned at extreme Downstage Right. On a table visible in foyer is a telephone with a very long extension cord. The front door is Offstage, Left of foyer. The stairs leading to the upper story are Offstage Right.*

AT RISE: *Morning SUNSHINE is slanting in through the street windows.* CHAPMAN, *the middle-aged colored butler, is discontentedly running a very modern-looking vacuum cleaner along the rug. Presently his niece,* SHIRLEY, *enters from the foyer.* SHIRLEY *is a pretty and mettlesome girl of nineteen, dressed in a becoming green-and-white morning uni-*

form. Like many persons of her age and sex, she walks (when she remembers) with just a shade more feminine allure than is strictly necessary for merely getting from place to place. At the moment, she carries a tray with orange juice, morning paper, etc. As she undulates across to a small table which is already partly laid for breakfast in the bar area:

CHAPMAN. (*Muttering.*) Up and down! Over and back! Wear the rug out! Cleanliness next to godliness! Gettin' so it's way up ahead of it nowadays! (*As the machine suddenly shudders and roars.*) Oh my! Throwed her fool belt again!

SHIRLEY. Watch yourself, Uncle Jesse.

CHAPMAN. Watch *whose* self!?

SHIRLEY. Whichever self is thinking all those sinful words!

CHAPMAN. (*Squatting over machine.*) It's *you* that's thinkin' sinful, to think *I'm* thinkin' sinful!

SHIRLEY. (*Drily.*) Ah-hn.—Should I set for two?

CHAPMAN. (*Nodding.*) Just in case.

SHIRLEY. Open these doors here?

CHAPMAN. (*Rising.*) No. He likes to do it himself. And don't get jelly on his *Times-Chronicle!* He knows if a body even looks at those headlines.

(*As* SHIRLEY *starts back toward the foyer with the now empty breakfast tray, she remembers to undulate.*)

CHAPMAN. (*Observing this.*) Shirley Lorraine, what are you doin' there!?

SHIRLEY. (*Stopping with dignity in entrance.*) Frankly, Uncle Jesse, I'm practicin' to walk stylish. A girl has to look out for her own future these days.

(CHAPMAN *watches her exit, resumes vacuuming.*)

CHAPMAN. (*A pious sigh.*) She ain't really *bad*, Lord. Just young. (*As machine suddenly roars again.*) *Oh my goodness GRACIOUS!*

(*As once more he drops to his knees,* EDITH STANNARD *enters unhurriedly into living room. She is in her early thirties, attractive and on her toes in the American manner, and just now wearing a smart house-coat, straight out of one of the ladies' magazines. During the following, she crosses to the breakfast table, makes minor rearrangements.*)

MRS. STANNARD. Well, good morning, Chapman! And why all the blue blazing blasphemy this fine morning?

CHAPMAN. (*A bit sheepish.*) Good morning, Miz Stannard. It's this new-model cleaner. It and me just don't take to each other.

MRS. STANNARD. (*Flinching*) Chapman! *What are you saying!?* Mr. Stannard has been tooling up on this model for six months. The new production schedule calls for a quarter of a million of them during the next fiscal period!

CHAPMAN. Fiscal or not, Miz Stannard, it has bugs in it!

MRS. STANNARD. *Bugs?* Are you mad!? (*Glancing toward entrance.*) At least keep your voice down!

CHAPMAN. (*Doggedly.*) Our old 1947 Hoover didn't throw her belt every time a man took off down the rug!

MRS. STANNARD. For pity's sake, Chapman! don't mention that name in this house! You'll get us both fired before breakfast!

CHAPMAN. (*As* BOTH *chuckle.*) Now Miz Stannard! the Boss couldn't get on without you and me. He's smart enough to know it, too.

MRS. STANNARD. You think? (*Before* CHAPMAN *can reply,* STANNARD *comes trotting down from stairs into living room. A man in his late thirties, vital and well set-up, he is shaved and combed, but his shirt-tail is out, and he carries his jacket and necktie as though under time pressure. The moment he appears,* MRS. STANNARD *starts the electric coffee pot and a toaster standing on the bar. Aside to* CHAPMAN.) *Get that thing out of sight!*

(CHAPMAN *hastily disconnects the vacuum, and is gathering the cord up as* STANNARD *tosses his jacket and necktie down on the sofa. He crosses, picks up the orange juice, jolts it in, stands glowering at* CHAPMAN.)

STANNARD. Old Man Sales Resistance! Against any model doesn't date back to the Stone Age! What are you trying to do here—sabotage me?

CHAPMAN. Me?

STANNARD. (*Opening machine.*) I could hear it upstairs! If you'd take the trouble to look inside, you've got this piece of string wrapped around the master pulley—keeps throwing the belt.

CHAPMAN. Yessir! (*Clutching the string and vacuum, he makes a fast, discreet exit.*)

STANNARD. (*Calling after him.*) That money-back guarantee ain't worth a hoot, if you don't follow the printed instructions! (*During the above,* MRS. STANNARD *has poured* STANNARD'S *cup of coffee, carefully creams and sugars it.*) That's a great little model we've got here! (*An exultant gesture.*) "Stannard sweeps the country!"

MRS. STANNARD. (*She shuts her eyes for a moment.*) I realize it's an inspired sales slogan dear, but honestly if I have to listen to it *just once more—!*

STANNARD. I know: You'll scream. That's what we want you to do! (*He takes a swallow of coffee, grins, puts his arm around her, and, very confident of himself, draws her close.*) Hi.

MRS. STANNARD. (*Fondly.*) You stinker. (STANNARD *is about to kiss her when the toast pops up, and she quickly has to butter it for him. Then she feeds him a huge bite, and watches him tie his necktie.*) Can't you sit down to it just for once?

STANNARD. (*His mouth full.*) Be late at the plant.

MRS. STANNARD. You'll get an ulcer, you know.

STANNARD. This country was built on ulcers.

MRS. STANNARD. But, Dave! After all, how much money do we *need?* I mean if you're planning an ocean-going yacht for your family, there just doesn't happen to *be* any ocean in these parts!

STANNARD. (*His necktie now tied, he starts tucking in his shirt-tails.*) You've been attending lectures.

MRS. STANNARD. Yes, I have, doggone it! The soul too must be fed!

STANNARD. Look—Edith! It's not just the profits for Stannard Brothers Incorporated. As of yesterday afternoon, we had 4827 people on the payroll. And that's not counting coast-to-coast agencies, or the Stannard TV hour.

MRS. STANNARD. Oh, yes! That dear, good Mr. Portalis! His hair is so slick, and he wears such beautiful sports jackets! And he's *so* sincere when he looks you in the eye, and says, "Stannard Vacuum is sweeping the country, friends!" (*She breaks off to scream attractively.*)

STANNARD. Believe it or not, George Portalis is a nice guy. (*Crossing toward his jacket.*) Why all the unholy quiet around here this morning? No cattle-rustlers, no space-bandits, no— (*Imitating a small boy imitating a machine-gun.*) eh-eh-eh-eh-eh-eh-eh!

MRS. STANNARD. (*Drily.*) Your son and heir rose as usual at five-twenty, tiptoed downstairs like an avalanche with rocks in it, and is now engaged in some frightful engineering project among my zinnias. Chapman barely managed to hurl some milk into him as he whizzed through.

STANNARD. Where do kids get that energy!

MRS. STANNARD. From the male parent, I dare say. (*Then softening.*) Davie's exactly like *you,* you know.

STANNARD. (*Ruefully grinning.*) Funny: When a woman tells her husband that, it's always supposed to be a compliment; but when she says it to the kid, she's getting set to whale the daylights out of him.

(*At this moment* CHAPMAN *re-enters rapidly with a covered dish.*)

CHAPMAN. Your bacon, sir. (STANNARD *removes the cover off the dish and pops a slice of bacon into his mouth with his fingers. Then he starts to put on his jacket.*) Let me help you, sir.

STANNARD. Thank you. (*A sudden grunt of pain.*) Ooch!

MRS. STANNARD. (*Sweetly.*) A twinge of conscience no doubt?

STANNARD. My bed last night: First the head tilts down, then the foot. (*With see-saw gestures.*) First the head—then the foot. All night.

MRS. STANNARD. But how spooky! Mine too—like something in an amusement park!

(CHAPMAN *glances thoughtfully from face to face, and starts to make a fast, unobtrusive exit.*)

STANNARD. Chapman.

CHAPMAN. (*Reluctantly stopping.*) Yessir?

STANNARD. How many slats to an old-style antique bed?

CHAPMAN. (*Stalling.*) On the average?

STANNARD. Yeah, on the average.

CHAPMAN. Well, sir, about three, sir.

STANNARD. How many do our beds have?

CHAPMAN. As of right now?

STANNARD. Right now!

CHAPMAN. Well, sir—on the average—about—one apiece.

STANNARD. (*Pondering, nodding.*) Uh-huh. (*He crosses rather grimly, slides the patio doors open, and all listen. Offstage there is a sound of uninhibited HAMMERING.*) That boy!

CHAPMAN. (*To himself.*) I don't even want to *be* here! (*He makes a fast exit, without glancing back.*)

STANNARD. (*Suddenly bawling Offstage.*) Davie! David!

A BOY'S VOICE. (*Cheerfully, Offstage.*) Yes, Daddy?

STANNARD. Never mind "Yes, Daddy!" Come in here—and that means *now!*

THE BOY'S VOICE. Don't flip your lid, Dad.

STANNARD. (*Bitterly aside.*) *Don't flip my lid!*
MRS. STANNARD. Now, Dave, he *is* exactly like you, you know!

(DAVIE STANNARD *appears in the garden doorway. He is seven-and-a-half years old [and accordingly smudged], dressed in shorts, sneakers, and T-shirt. He carries a hammer, and what all too obviously are a couple of bed-slats, nailed together askew.*)

DAVIE. (*Genially off-hand.*) Hi, Mom. Hi, Dad.
STANNARD. (*Still grim.*) Tell me just one thing: How did you lift those heavy springs on all eight beds?
DAVIE. We didn't. We just sort of slid up in under, and give these things a big twist, and they drop right out for us.
STANNARD. I ought to give *you* a big twist! I— (*Interrupting himself.*) Who is "we"?
DAVIE. Me and Butch Bissel. Today though he got walloped and kep' home for getting us door-hinges.
MRS. STANNARD. Very sound people, the Bissels.

(DAVIE *has put the bed-slats down on the floor, and begins inexpertly hammering more nails in.* STANNARD *watches.*)

STANNARD. That's no way to use a hammer. (*Taking over.*) Here. You hold it way down by the end of the handle—see? Now keep your eye on the nail. (*He hits his own thumb. Muffled curses as he nurses and sucks it.*)
DAVIE. (*Retrieving hammer.*) That's the way *I* did when I first begun. (*Looking proudly Offstage.*) Wait till you see this deal when we're finished. Keen, huh?
MRS. STANNARD. Yes! What is it?
DAVIE. (*Coldly superior.*) It's our fort, of course. It's even going to have a roof. (*Gloomily shaking his head.*) We're way short on planks, though.
STANNARD. (*Rather bitter.*) There's still the family ironing board—or the leaves out of your mother's dining table.

DAVIE. (*Brightening.*) Gai! That'll do it!

MRS. STANNARD. (*Hastily.*) No, no! That was supposed to be a very funny joke, dear.

(*As* DAVIE'S *face falls, an AUTOMOBILE HORN begins sounding in the street outside.*)

STANNARD. There's your school bus.

DAVIE. (*Promptly starting.*) Okay!

MRS. STANNARD. Wait! You can't go like that! (*To* STANNARD.) Hold him right here—I'll get him a clean shirt.

(*She disappears into foyer toward stairs on the dead run, and* STANNARD *and* DAVIE *are left alone together near entrance. A slight awkwardness comes over them.*)

STANNARD. So you're short of lumber—huh?

DAVIE. (*Gravely.*) Yep.

STANNARD. I'll try to pick you up some on my way home.

DAVIE. *Buy* it? That wouldn't be any fun, Daddy.

STANNARD. (*Secretly tickled.*) Ethics, hm? Well, I—I'll swipe you some, then. (*Finishing coffee.*) Tell you what: I'll break away somehow this afternoon. Meet you here right after school.

DAVIE. (*He stands incredulous, moved almost to tears.*) You'll really make my fort with me, Daddy!?

STANNARD. Sure. We'll figure out some kind of a door for it.

DAVIE. (*Suddenly grabs his father's legs, and hugs hard with both arms.*) Gai! I bet there isn't many fathers would leave their own business for just their kid!

STANNARD. (*Now* STANNARD *is moved too. He touches the boy's hair awkwardly.*) So far, I'm afraid I've sinned mostly in the other direction.

DAVIE. Huh?

(*The AUTOMOBILE HORN blares insistently again,*

and simultaneously MRS. STANNARD *comes running back with* DAVIE'S *fresh T-shirt.*)

MRS. STANNARD. It's simply incredible—*just one left!* Night before last you couldn't get the drawer shut. And it isn't as though he ever looks really *clean!*

(*As she arrives,* STANNARD *pulls the soiled shirt off over* DAVIE'S *head with a single motion.*)

DAVIE. Ooch, my ears!
STANNARD. It's all right. Now they get pulled the other way.

(MRS. STANNARD *whips the clean shirt on* DAVIE *to an accompaniment of further "ooches." The whole process rather suggests a team conjuring act. The shirt itself is largely white, with a narrow red-white-and-blue band around the middle.*)

MRS. STANNARD. White! I hate to think what it will look like by tonight.

(*The AUTOMOBILE HORN is now having hysterics.* STANNARD *watches, while* MRS. STANNARD *tucks the shirt inside* DAVIE'S *shorts.*)

STANNARD. (*To* DAVIE.) Just for the record: Are you the dirtiest boy in your school?
DAVIE. No, Butchie Bissell is the dirtiest. I'm only second dirtiest.
MRS. STANNARD. (*Slapping* DAVIE'S *bottom.*) There we are! (*As he heads for foyer.*) Davie!
DAVIE. (*Stopping for kiss.*) Aw, Mom!
MRS. STANNARD. Now run along. Mrs. Partridge doesn't like the children to be late.
DAVIE. (*As he dashes out.*) Don't forget after school, Dad!
STANNARD. (*Calling after him.*) Don't *you* forget!

(*The* STANNARDS *wince slightly as the front door SLAMS —then move together to the front windows, and look out. There is a sound of the school BUS driving off down the street, and finally the* STANNARDS *turn back, and smile ruefully at each other.*) Well, Edith, at least we've only got the one.

MRS. STANNARD. (*Comically clutching her head.*) Don't even bring it up!

(*Before either can say more,* CHAPMAN *enters.*)

CHAPMAN. Your car's in the driveway, sir.

(STANNARD *glances at his watch, grunts in consternation, goes into foyer, grabs his hat off the table. As* CHAPMAN *exits past him, Right.*)

STANNARD. (*To* MRS. STANNARD.) See you at dinner—
MRS. STANNARD. Just a minute, Thunderbolt!
STANNARD. Well, come and get it! I'm late at the plant this minute! (*He exits toward Right.*)
MRS. STANNARD. (*Hurrying after him.*) When a woman has to chase a man for a kiss, she knows she's right in her own home!

(*She exits.* SHIRLEY *and* CHAPMAN *enter.* SHIRLEY *begins gathering up the soiled T-shirt and the breakfast things.*)

CHAPMAN. (*Chuckling, as he looks out into garden.*) That old shack he's got out there, a person wouldn't keep a goat in it.

CURTAIN

END OF SCENE 1

ACT ONE

Scene 2

SCENE: *4 P. M. the same afternoon. SUNLIGHT now pours in through the patio doors.*

AT RISE: *MRS. STANNARD enters slowly. She is dressed charmingly for the afternoon. She pauses at entrance, looking about the room, then crosses to a window and looks out. After a moment CHAPMAN enters, starts distributing clean ash trays.*

CHAPMAN. Oh—excuse me. I didn't know you were in here, Miz Stannard.

MRS. STANNARD. I'm expecting Mr. Stannard home early.

CHAPMAN. Yes, ma'am.

(*He crosses to the bar, steps behind the counter, quickly assembles the makings for highballs, finally coming out with a tray which he sets on a table with the air of established ritual. Simultaneously, MRS. STANNARD sits down at the spinet, tinkles idly for a few moments, but when CHAPMAN silently makes his exit, she stops, lights herself a cigarette, and then starts playing with unexpected power and majesty. Suddenly she breaks off, sits listening. There is the sound of a CAR DOOR slamming Offstage. MRS. STANNARD stands up, snubbing out her cigarette, and hurries like a girl to answer the front door. As she goes into the foyer the door, Off Left, is slowly bumped open. She looks toward it, puzzled. STANNARD comes into view, maneuvering a load of several ancient planks, dusty with plaster, and spattered with paint, with some difficulty. As they come into living room MRS. STANNARD snatches a handsome glass bowl out of harm's way.*)

MRS. STANNARD. David! Liz and Ed's wedding-present!

STANNARD. (*Cheerily.*) Yeah, what would Freud say!

MRS. STANNARD. (*Retreating ahead of him.*) Never mind about Freud. You can't bring those filthy things into my living room!

STANNARD. Construction materials. (*Dumping the planks into sofa.*) Grand larceny at the site of the new Commercial Building.

MRS. STANNARD. Sometimes I'm obliged to remind myself that all male creatures are certifiably insane.

STANNARD. Sure—because our wives and mothers are usually women— (*Kissing her cheek.*) thank the good Lord!

(*The kiss has been too perfunctory for* MRS. STANNARD's *taste. Faintly sulky, she sits down at the spinet, starts doing finger exercises.*)

MRS. STANNARD. *Larceny?* Nice headlines in the *Times-Chronicle!*

STANNARD. It's okay. I slipped the honest foreman five bucks. He wanted to throw in twenty yards of copper tubing. (*Suddenly anxious.*) Don't let Davie know I double-crossed him, though! It seems to jam up the kid's ethics if the stuff isn't a hundred percent stolen goods.

MRS. STANNARD. Nice example *you're* giving! No—don't laugh, Dave! It isn't funny! A child can't distinguish between big and little. And if his own parents don't teach him citizenship—!

(STANNARD *sits down on the piano bench with her, pulls her close.*)

STANNARD. Why are you always so attractive when you get righteous?

MRS. STANNARD. (*As he kisses her.*) Well! (*Singing operatically.*) "Stannard is sweeping the country—"

STANNARD. (*Still kissing.*) Didn't know you cared.

(*He pulls her into a really big embrace—and this puts her back into good humor.*)

MRS. STANNARD. I wish you'd come home two hours early *every* day! It's usually— (*A gruff parody of* STANNARD.) "When do we eat, kid?" (*Gaily rising.*) I'll fix you a drink, and see just where all this will lead to!

STANNARD. (*Grabbing her.*) Wait a minute. (*This time his kiss is far from perfunctory.*)

MRS. STANNARD. (*Becoming uneasy.*) Chapman might come in!

STANNARD. Do him good—broaden his outlook.

MRS. STANNARD. (*Somewhat breathless.*) Dave! What on earth has come over you at this time of day!?

STANNARD. (*Still kissing.*) Don't bother me! I'm just beginning to catch on why the unemployed always have such big families. (*Gradually* MRS. STANNARD's *arms encircle him, and she has really begun to respond, when* STANNARD *suddenly releases her.*) Where is he?

MRS. STANNARD. Who?

STANNARD. Him.

MRS. STANNARD. (*Arranging her hair.*) Oh. Not home yet.

STANNARD. (*When this has sunk in, he puts down the cigarette he has started to light, peers puzzledly at her.*) What are you talking about! The school bus was pulling away from the Bissels' just as I turned into our street.

MRS. STANNARD. (*Frowning.*) You're sure? (*As* STANNARD *nods.*) The little demon's run off somewhere. (*Starting to pace.*) He knows perfectly well he's supposed to check in before he goes anyplace! Remember last March? For three mortal hours I waited to hear he'd been run over by some truck.

STANNARD. (*His face has fallen slowly. He stands with his hands in his pockets, smiling down sourly at the pile of planks on the sofa.*) He and I had a date to finish building that fool shack.

MRS. STANNARD. (*Soothing.*) Oh, Dave, he's only seven years old—he must have forgotten all about it.

STANNARD. Sure. He forgot all about it. (*Snapping.*) Anyway, he's nearly *eight* years old! (*He turns away abruptly, walks to the table, pours himself a straight one, and jolts it in.*)

MRS. STANNARD. If you do that every time you lose your temper, you'll turn into an alcoholic.

STANNARD. I haven't *time* to be an alcoholic! (*Staring bitterly into his glass.*) "Share your children's hobbies," says The Board of Education. (*As TELEPHONE rings in foyer.*) So I kick my way out of a production meeting, and leave the whole plant on its ear, and what do I get for it—!

(*As the TELEPHONE rings again,* CHAPMAN *enters.*)

CHAPMAN. (*Answering telephone.*) The Stannard residence. . . . Yes, ma'am— I'll see. Just one minute, please. (*He comes into living room, carrying the telephone on its long extension cord, his hand over the mouthpiece.*) For you, Ma'am. Miz Partridge at the school.

STANNARD. (*Brightening.*) Sure! The kid's been kept in.

(MRS. STANNARD *takes the telephone, sits down with it on arm of sofa as* CHAPMAN *exits.*)

MRS. STANNARD. Mrs. Partridge? . . . Yes, this is Edith Stannard. . . . Very well, thank you.—And you? . . . Splendid! . . . Yes, hasn't it!—just pleasantly warm. (*Then she is listening to something she does not quite follow, and from this point forward she becomes, in a polite way, increasingly bewildered.* STANNARD *decides to make himself another drink, while unsuccessfully trying to keep track of the conversation.*) I beg your pardon? . . . I'm sorry, Mrs. Partridge, I didn't quite . . . Dr. Gorman's *nurse?* But how extraordinary! Did the child seem to feel badly? (*As* STANNARD *stops pouring drink.*) Oh. . . . I see! . . . No, Mrs. Partridge, I most certainly had *not* heard. But perhaps my husband was afraid that if he told me . . . Oh, no! I'm sure if it were something contagious . . . Yes, I quite understand your position. And personally, I'm delighted you take such an interest. . . . Yes, I shall, Mrs. Partridge. I'll certainly call you right back. (*She hangs up slowly, remains frowning slightly.*) That's the most peculiar thing I ever heard in my life!

STANNARD. *What* is!? Come on—give!

MRS. STANNARD. (*Still puzzling.*) It seems Dr. Gorman sent his nurse for Davie in a taxi about eleven this morning.

STANNARD. (*Plaintively bewildered.*) Gorman!? *To the school?* But why? What for?

MRS. STANNARD. (*Still puzzled, rising.*) It seems the laboratory tests came through. Dr. Gorman thought Davie ought to be brought down to his office right away. (*A sudden jump in her voice.*) Dave! It's been five hours.

STANNARD. Laboratory tests? Look, Edith—you ought to keep me posted on these things.

MRS. STANNARD. You don't know, either? Now, Dave! If you're keeping something back—!

STANNARD. *Me!?* I'm never told anything! I just work around here. (*He grabs the telephone, starts dialing irritably.*)

MRS. STANNARD. Mrs. Partridge seemed rather concerned that it might be polio.

STANNARD. (*His face flashes around toward her—then he relaxes.*) He's had his shots! That isn't how polio strikes, anyway. (*As telephone is answered.*) Hello? D. G. Stannard calling. Let me speak to the doctor, please. (*Aside, as he waits.*) People are so blamed off-hand about other people's kids— (*Into telephone.*) Hi, Doc! It's Dave Stannard. (*Ready to laugh things off now.*) What have you been doing to that boy of ours—trying to repossess him on us? (*Listening—a bewildered look coming into his face.*) Huh? . . . You've still got him there, haven't you? . . . Come again, Doc? . . . But that snooty nurse of yours . . . she picked him up at school before lunch. . . . No, I'm not clowning—are you? . . . Oh. . . . He hasn't? . . . No, in a taxi. . . . What's that? . . . Wait a minute— (*Turning to* MRS. STANNARD.) Was she in uniform?

MRS. STANNARD. Who?

STANNARD. The nurse! The nurse!

MRS. STANNARD. Yes—Partridge mentioned a white uniform with a cap.

STANNARD. (*There is deep, controlled fright in* STANNARD'S *manner now. From this point onward it rushes through the secret canyons of his mind like a flash flood. Quietly into telephone.*) Yep, white uniform with a cap. . . . Yep. . . . Does sort of look like it, doesn't it? . . . Yeah. . . . Sure, I'll call. . . . (*Glancing at his wife.*) Just a second, Doc! I want you to get up here in nothing flat! (*He hangs up softly, stands looking at her.*)

MRS. STANNARD. Dave! *What's the matter?*

STANNARD. (*Takes both her hands firmly in his.*) Sit down, Edith. You've got to take a very big grip on yourself.

(*She sits down frightenedly, and he drops to one knee before her, still gripping her hands.*)

MRS. STANNARD. What do you mean?

STANNARD. Davie isn't at Gorman's office . . . hasn't been there all day.

MRS. STANNARD. But that nurse! She—

STANNARD. *She wasn't a nurse, Edith.*

MRS. STANNARD. (*For a moment* MRS. STANNARD'S *mind gropes. Then suddenly her whole body tenses with understanding. Eerie and quiet.*) *Oh God!* They've stolen him! Our boy—!

STANNARD. (*Gripping her hands.*) Listen!—listen to me! As long as we've been married, have I ever lied to you, or broken my word? (*She stares at him with her teeth chattering—shakes her head vaguely in reply.*) All right then, Edith. Right here I swear to God and to you that we'll get Davie back! (*He stands up, gently releasing her, and she remains seated, twisting her hands together, her face drawn. Watching her anxiously,* STAN-

NARD *lifts the telephone again, and dials "O."*) Operator?
—This is an emergency. I want the Chief of Police.
(*At these words, some fuller realization seems to sweep through* EDITH STANNARD, *and a hoarse sound is forced out of her throat.* STANNARD *winces and glares.*) Edith!
(*She stifles the guilty sound, clutching her mouth childishly with both hands, and sits, large-eyed, watching* STANNARD *without further movement or sound. Tensely on telephone.*) Chief Horgan?—D. J. Stannard speaking, 1411 Summit Avenue. I have reason to believe that my son Davie was kidnapped from the Covey Lane Day School at approximately 11 o'clock this morning—

CURTAIN

END OF SCENE 2

ACT ONE

SCENE 3

SCENE: *11 o'clock that night. All the lights are on in foyer and living room, with a total impression of glowing elegance. By contrast, the old, dirty planks on the sofa are somehow sinister and cockeyed. The telephone stands on an end table near the sofa. Curtains are drawn across the open patio doors.*

AT RISE: *The Stage is empty, and the front DOORBELL is ringing faintly but steadily. After several moments,* CHAPMAN *enters hurriedly in foyer, from Right, crosses to open the door. A rawboned, moustached, gray-haired man enters quickly, followed by* CHAPMAN.

CHAPMAN. (*Bristling.*) Just hold on now, mister! What *you* want pushin' in here!? (*Belated recognition.*) Oh—Chief Horgan! I didn't know you without the uniform.

The mister is upstairs in Miz Stannard's room with the doctor.

THE CHIEF. Want to talk to you first. (*As he herds* CHAPMAN *into the living room ahead of him, the* CHIEF *reveals a slight, characteristic limp, as though some mishap of long ago had left one of his legs slightly shorter than the other.*) How many of you people in the kitchen?

CHAPMAN. Just me and the maid—she's my sister's youngest.

THE CHIEF. Nobody else?

CHAPMAN. Well, sometimes for special we have in my cousin's husband, and his mother-in-law, and— (*Suddenly tremulous.*) The mister's already telephoned to call off the party for tomorrow—without lettin' on to any of 'em, that is.

THE CHIEF. (*Impressed.*) He handled that himself?

CHAPMAN. Yes, sir.

THE CHIEF. Now listen: You haven't seen me here tonight—understand? And get this: Any blabbing right now could make you an accessory in this thing.

CHAPMAN. (*With dignity.*) You got no call to say that to me, mister! I've buttled this family since before little Mr. Davie was borned. I've carried him in my arms—he's throwed up on my white coat here—!

(*During the above,* SHIRLEY *has quietly entered the foyer behind them. She stands in entrance, looking from one to the other, hollow-eyed, somber.*)

SHIRLEY. What's he want?

(*Both* MEN *turn abruptly toward her.*)

THE CHIEF. This the niece?

(CHAPMAN *nods.*)

SHIRLEY. (*To* CHIEF.) Was a white woman took him. This ain't any colored crime, mister—this a *white* crime! You know it, too.

CHAPMAN. Shirley, you get back in the kitchen.

SHIRLEY. That what he comin' round us for! (*To* CHIEF.) Always got to be a black man, ain't it! Black booger-man. Try an' hang it on us.—This a *white* crime! You can't do this way, mister—startin' race-trouble in this town!

CHAPMAN. (*Gentle but firm.*) Shirley Lorraine, you just go to your room. Hear me now?

SHIRLEY. (*Suddenly her somber dignity collapses—she is simply a crying girl.*) I'm sorry! But that cute, nice little boy—I just can't stand it, Uncle Jesse—I can't! (*She turns, and exits quickly.*)

THE CHIEF. (*He unbuttons his overcoat without taking it off, turns away down the room.*) Sorry I spoke that way—kind of shook up. In a thing like this, any kid is everybody's kid.

CHAPMAN. (*His eye is caught by the plaster-spattered boards in the sofa. Crossing.*) Let me get these out of here—

(*During the above,* STANNARD *comes briskly into the foyer just as* CHAPMAN *picks the boards up.* STANNARD *is haggard, but in essentials* he is still the same man.)

STANNARD. (*Sharply to* CHAPMAN *as he comes into living room.*) Leave those! Stand 'em there in the corner—I want the boy to see them first thing when he gets home. (*The* CHIEF *gives* STANNARD *a covertly thoughtful glance. During the following,* CHAPMAN *very carefully stands the boards up against the wall between the bar and the patio doors, then unobtrusively makes his exit. Coming down the three steps.*) You know, Chief? I figure we've been watched for a long time—

THE CHIEF. (*As they shake hands.*) Anything since we talked?

STANNARD. Not a thing. You?

THE CHIEF. (*Evasive.*) Little soon yet. In these cases we always get set on certain routine things, and then—stand by.

STANNARD. (*He stands thinking about this.*) *Always?
. . . Routine!?*

THE CHIEF. Have you got any serious family problems, Mr. Stannard?

STANNARD. Not this kind!

THE CHIEF. Business beefs? Big personal enemies?

STANNARD. Half a dozen. But they'd take my shirt, not my son.

THE CHIEF. (*Removing overcoat.*) This could be quite a wait. These people usually let the family sweat blood for a while.

STANNARD. Then you feel certain the motive is—

THE CHIEF. Mr. Stannard! Nothing about this is certain till that telephone rings, or we receive something in the mail. Maybe not then for sure.

STANNARD. You don't feel like letting me know what measures are being taken?

THE CHIEF. In my opinion it's better if you and your good wife ain't in on everything at this state. We—we're dealing with a capital offense here. (*He moves away across the room. For a moment his limp is slightly accentuated. Turning back.*) One thing you can depend on, though, Mr. Stannard: We aren't going to jeopardize any arrangements you may feel like making on your own responsibility as the boy's father.

STANNARD. (*A shadow of puzzlement.*) I more or less expected to take directions.

THE CHIEF. (*Eluding this.*) Fact is, I talked to the Mayor just before I come up here, and he said to me, "Jim, you tell those two poor people that this Administration is with them right down the line—and that's official!"

(*Suddenly, the TELEPHONE rings. Both MEN wheel, and stare at it, unable to move for a moment. It rings a second time, but as they start forward together, CHAPMAN is already coming into the living room.*)

CHAPMAN. (*Answering telephone.*) The Stannard residence. . . . Yes sir, he's right here. Just one moment. (*Handing telephone to Stannard.*) Your brother, sir. Calling from the Golf Club.

STANNARD. (*Eagerly into telephone.*) Al? Is the door to your booth shut? Yes, it's true, all right—just like Edith told Liz. . . . No, from the Day School. . . . Well, how do you suppose she is! Gorman's with her. . . . Come over? Absolutely not! We're waiting here for a contact. Just stand by till we call you.—And, Al! Don't talk—not to anybody. Now do you get that? Talk to *nobody!* . . . Sure, thanks, kid. I'll call you the minute we hear anything.

(*As he hangs up,* MRS. STANNARD *comes into living room accompanied by an elderly and worried* DR. GORMAN. MRS. STANNARD *is wearing the smart housecoat again—but now it is buttoned wrong, her hair is in some disorder, and her expression is glazed from sedatives. During all the following, her hands never quite leave off fretting at each other.*)

MRS. STANNARD. Oh, please, Dr. Gorman! I'm quite able to manage. If the Chief is here, there are several things I want to take up with him.

DR. GORMAN. Dave, this bad girl of yours won't give in to my barbiturates. I've been telling her we may have to bring in a nurse—

MRS. STANNARD. *Nurse?* I won't have a nurse! (STANNARD *and* DR. GORMAN *both wince slightly. Without looking at them,* MRS. STANNARD *crosses to* THE CHIEF.) Chief Horgan?

THE CHIEF. Yes, ma'am.

MRS. STANNARD. Have you located him?

THE CHIEF. Not yet, ma'am.

MRS. STANNARD. Why not! That's your job, isn't it? It's what you're paid for!

THE CHIEF. We're trying to handle this the very best way, ma'am.

DR. GORMAN. (*Aside to* STANNARD.) See if you can coax her upstairs—I'll give her a real shot.

MRS. STANNARD. (*Still to* THE CHIEF.) But what possible good can you be doing *here?* I mean this would certainly be the very last place—!

STANNARD. (*Quietly grasping her elbows.*) Please sit down, Edith.

(*She seems really to see him for the first time, and for a moment her normal personality comes through mistily. She limply allows him to seat her in the sofa.*)

MRS. STANNARD. Poor dear Dave. This is so terrible for you—your only son. (*To* THE CHIEF *again.*) Don't you see? He's got to be brought back tonight—*this evening!* He's never been away from home—he'll be frightened! Not even his toothbrush, or his own little nightclothes—! (*The three* MEN *stand looking down at her, helpless and wretched. But suddenly she is smiling.*) Do you remember, Dave? It snowed all the day before, and then it thawed, but that night it froze hard, and the afternoon he was born, all the trees in town were covered with diamonds—like an honor, like a great wonderful promise! And just at sunset, they brought him in for the first time, and left him with me.

THE CHIEF. (*With a sudden, silencing gesture.*) Hold it! (*His eyes are fixed on the drawn curtains before the open patio doors. Suddenly* THE CHIEF'S *gun is in his fist. Advancing, slow and watchful.*) O.K. Come on in. And nothin' cute—hear? (*A* MAN *steps carefully into view from behind the curtains. He is in his late forties, and wears a rumpled topcoat, and a studiedly beat-up hat, beneath which his face is likably shrewd, cynical, and tough.* THE CHIEF *disgustedly shoves the gun back into his shoulder holster.*) Charlie! For Pete's sake, how did you latch onto this one!

CHARLIE. (*Looking around the room.*) All the reserves out? —Big hush on the police switchboard?—Mayor's office lit up like a juke-box? Then *you* take out in plain clothes! You think I don't chase *that* up!?

STANNARD. Who *is* this man?

THE CHIEF. (*Apologetic.*) A friend of mine, Mr. Stannard. Meet Charlie Telfer of *The Times-Chronicle*.

STANNARD. You mean—*headlines!?*

THE CHIEF. (*Soothing.*) Now, this can be handled.

STANNARD. But it's the first thing you warned me over the telephone—*no publicity!—nobody must be told anything!* (*Turning on* CHARLIE.) On your way before I run you out personally! And this time the *front* door will do!

CHARLIE. (*Unruffled.*) Never threaten The Press, Stannard—even when you're in pain. (*As* THE CHIEF *puts a restraining grip on* STANNARD'S *biceps,* CHARLIE *for the first time observes* MRS. STANNARD, *as she sits looking vaguely at him. After a moment, he removes his hat, revealing a mop of unkempt, iron-gray hair. He drops the hat into a chair.*) You gents don't really figure to keep a thing like this covered, do you? Look where it's known already: Right here—at that school—down at Headquarters and City Hall—probably all over the exchange by now—— (*A grimly significant look.*) and at least one other place—huh? (*He spots a silver-framed photograph of* DAVIE *on the mantelpiece. He picks it up, stands looking at it.*) This the boy?

MRS. STANNARD. (*With controlled pride.*) Of course he's only six years and seven months in that photograph—he's grown tremendously.

CHARLIE. (*Still studying the photograph.*) I'll need this.

(*He turns it over, and starts unfastening the back of the frame.* STANNARD *can hardly believe his own senses for a moment.*)

STANNARD. (*Furious.*) Put it down!

(CHARLIE *only gives him a bored glance, opens the frame and takes the photograph out.* THE CHIEF *expertly grabs* STANNARD, *hangs onto his arm again.*)

The Chief. You'll have to take it, and like it, Mr. Stannard! (*After a moment or two* Stannard *very reluctantly knuckles under.*) Just the same, Charlie! if your sheet breaks this, every crank and chiseler this side of the Mississippi will be ringing that telephone!—and no way on earth of telling which one of them really has the boy.

Charlie. (*Slips the photograph into his pocket.*) The policy of our paper will be to hold off till you get your contact. But, Chief! (*Smiling coldly, wagging forefinger.*) Don't let anybody beat us with this story—like one of your boys figuring he might as well pick up a smart twenty-five bucks from one of the wire-services. You could come out of this one with your shield bent—you know that, don't you?

Stannard. You cold-blooded hoodlum!

Charlie. (*Turning on him.*) Why don't you quit climbing me, Stannard! What do you want me to do, draw you a diagram? *My paper is on your kid's side!* We want to see him back in his mother's arms, just like you do!

(*During the above,* Chapman *has appeared quietly at entrance.*)

Chapman. Should I show this gentleman the door, sir?

Charlie. Well! Sugar Ray in person!—or is it Uncle Tom? (*As he thus confirms a mutual and permanent hostility, the TELEPHONE rings again. Once more* All *start, and wheel toward it. Snatching telephone.*) The Stannard home! (*Losing interest.*) Oh. . . . Sheriff's office.

The Chief. (*Taking telephone.*) Jake? . . . What's that? . . . No, no, I *told* you—a plain white, size eight T-shirt. Just a narrow red-white-and-blue band around it. . . . Yeah—seventy pounds, give or take a couple. . . . That's right—first molars, and all second incisors . . . canines and bicuspids either part grown or missing. . . . Huh? (*Turning to* Stannard.) Any blemishes or distinguishing marks?

MRS. STANNARD. Davie? Certainly not!

STANNARD. (*Hopefully.*) Freckles!

THE CHIEF. (*Into telephone.*) Prominent freckles, Jake. . . . Huh? . . . Well, as far as I know, they show up in either case. The Coroner's office can tell you. Listen, Jake! Have your boys go real careful, will you? We want that kid back, and if anybody gets these people feelin' nervous . . . Come again? . . . The Federals?—No, so far I've just notified. They're on stand-by. . . . Right, Jake. If I'm not here, I'll be back at headquarters.

CHARLIE. (*As* THE CHIEF *hangs up.*) What's the idea of holding off the F. B. I.? Want all the bows?

THE CHIEF. You know me better than that, Charlie.

CHARLIE. I don't know *anybody* better than that! (*Prowling the room.*) Anyway, under the Lindbergh Law, they can move in after the first week without an invitation.

MRS. STANNARD. (*Sitting up—ghostly.*) The first—week?

CHARLIE. (*Defensively.*) Just a technical point.

(*But now the TELEPHONE is ringing again—and once more* CHARLIE *is there first.*)

STANNARD. I'll take that!

(CHARLIE *shrugs, relinquishes it.*)

THE CHIEF. (*Aside to* CHARLIE.) Will you behave yourself!?

STANNARD. (*On telephone.*) D. J. Stannard speaking! (*As he listens, his face falls. He hands the telephone to* THE CHIEF, *and* ALL *the others relax again. To* CHIEF.) One of your men.

THE CHIEF. (*On telephone.*) Hello. . . . Yes, Danny. . . . I see. . . . Anyway, run a routine check. (*Hanging up.*) Every known con woman who could fit that nurse description is in the clear—so it can't be regular professionals. . . . (*Reluctantly.*) Sure was a nicely planned job, though.

CHARLIE. (*He sits down as though he were tired.*) But the plan itself still rules out any straight psycho angle. (*To* STANNARD.) And you can be glad of that, mister!

MRS. STANNARD. I beg your pardon?

STANNARD. (*Hastily.*) Edith, we've got to expect a certain amount of shop-talk.

MRS. STANNARD. (*She has hardly heard him. She is off again, thinking on her own. Softly and suddenly.*) I don't believe any of this for a minute. She must have seen Davie somewhere. Everybody always takes notice of him. It's only natural, poor woman, with no little boy of her own. The thing is, we must get in touch with her—let her know everything's perfectly all right. Matter of fact, she's quite free to come and visit with the child whenever she wishes. Only she must bring him home at once—tonight, do you understand me? (*Breaking.*) *Now! Now! Now! Now!*

STANNARD. (*In cold suffering.*) Get her upstairs to bed, Doctor.

MRS. STANNARD. (*Controlling herself.*) No! Please! I'll be good. I won't say a word. I'll sit here. (*Losing it again—rising.*) All of you! Not doing a single thing—making speeches! You especially, Dave Stannard—his own father! Don't you know what they do? They do all sorts of things to them. Then they make you listen to it on the telephone. My son! My loving little boy—!

DR. GORMAN. (*Moving toward her.*) Edith! Edith! Be a good girl. It's time for that nap. You promised—!

CHAPMAN. (*As he and* STANNARD *also close in.*) This isn't like you, Miss Edith. It isn't like you for a single minute.

CHARLIE. (*Suddenly.*) Hey—listen! The front door—

(ALL *stop where they are; their heads turn together. A steady* KNOCKING *is audible, and, more faintly, insistent blasts of the* DOORBELL. STANNARD *glances questioningly at* THE CHIEF, *who shrugs noncommittally.*)

STANNARD. (*To* CHAPMAN.) If it's a caller, get rid of them.

(*As* CHAPMAN *exits toward front door,* MRS. STANNARD *sees her opportunity like a sly child. She slips back into her place on the sofa.*)

CHAPMAN. (*Offstage—a note of recognition.*) Oh, good evening, ma'am. The family isn't home right now.
A WOMAN'S VOICE. (*With brisk assurance.*) Nonsense, Chapman! I know better.
CHAPMAN. (*Off.*) Sorry, ma'am, but that's my instructions.
THE WOMAN'S VOICE. (*Off.*) Instructions don't apply in my case—now stand aside like a sensible fellow.

(*A* LADY, *perhaps 50 years old, appears at entrance. She is smart and slim in imported tweeds, and with trim ankles and a still piquant profile. A small beret is dragged down over one side of her blue-rinsed gray hair, and she moves confidently and elegantly.*)

STANNARD. Mrs. Partridge!
MRS. PARTRIDGE. (*Coming into living room.*) Don't worry, Mr. Stannard—I've already seen the police, and know exactly what's expected of me. (*Turning to* MRS. STANNARD.) Mrs. Stannard! What a dreadful, dreadful day this has been for all of us! Such a bright, promising little boy! If there's anything I can possibly do—
STANNARD. (*Quietly interposing.*) We appreciate your concern, Mrs. Partridge, but right now we're waiting for a contact. Naturally, any unusual amount of coming or going here tonight—
MRS. PARTRIDGE. I quite understand. (*Turning to* THE CHIEF.) As it happened, I was in conference this morning, but fortunately Miss Belding, our drawing instructress, caught a glimpse of the woman. She's down at the station house now, trying to reconstruct the face from memory.

STANNARD. (*He glances over at* MRS. STANNARD. *His jaw sets.*) Mrs. Partridge, if you'll arrange to call again in a day or two—

MRS. PARTRIDGE. (*Hurt and astonished.*) Well! I certainly didn't expect *this* attitude!

STANNARD. (*He closes his eyes.*) No attitude. Mrs. Stannard and I don't hold you in any way responsible.

MRS. PARTRIDGE. (*Her eyes widen in outrage.*) Responsible! *Responsible!?* I'm sure *nobody* could have given the child more devoted care than I and my girls! After all, Dr. Gorman is your family physician—there he is, right there! And the woman *did* present herself as his nurse, you know! After all, Mr. Stannard, *I've* been victimized, too, by this.

CHARLIE. (*Softly.*) Now I've heard everything.

MRS. PARTRIDGE. (*Wheeling.*) And who is this young man?

CHARLIE. (*A mocking nod.*) *Times-Chronicle.*

MRS. PARTRIDGE. *A reporter!?* (*Instantly all her hard aggressiveness is in plain view. To* CHARLIE.) I wish it clearly understood that if you or anyone else should give out the least bit of adverse publicity regarding Covey Lane Junior Day School, I shall be obliged to put the whole matter into the hands of our attorneys.

MRS. STANNARD. (*She suddenly stands up. Deadly quiet.*) Get out of my house.

MRS. PARTRIDGE. (*Gasping.*) What an extraordinary—

(EDITH STANNARD *reaches behind her, grasps the fireplace poker.*)

MRS. STANNARD. (*One step forward.*) Get out!

(MRS. PARTRIDGE *turns, and scuttles into foyer, bouncing slightly, with* CHAPMAN *right at her heels.*)

MRS. PARTRIDGE. I call on all of you to witness these threats!

(*She flounces out toward front door.* CHAPMAN *follows her, slamming the front door behind her. Simultaneously, the* TELEPHONE *rings, but nobody heeds it this time.* MRS. STANNARD *drops the poker with a clatter, sits down in the sofa again, covers her face with her hands, and begins sobbing softly. As* CHAPMAN *returns,* STANNARD *grabs the telephone in absent-minded exasperation.*)

STANNARD. Hullo!—Huh? . . . Who? What's that again? *Who* did you say? (*As he listens, his face changes. He lifts his hand formidably for silence. One by one the others realize that this at last is contact.* ALL *remain in arrested postures, eyes fixed on* STANNARD'S *face. During the following,* MRS. STANNARD *crosses, with her hands tensely clasped, as though she were about to fall on her knees before telephone. Careful and quiet.*) Yes. . . . Yes, I understand now. . . . Go ahead, please. I can hear you perfectly. . . . Hm-hm. . . . Hm-hm. . . . One moment! May I talk to the boy? . . . Why not? . . . Tell me the color of his eyes, then. . . . Now describe his clothing, please. (*As he listens to each answer, he looks across at* THE CHIEF, *and nods gravely and affirmatively.*) Beg pardon? . . . Very well—hold on a second. (*Sharp and anxious.*) It's no trap!—I tell you I'm *not* stalling! Simply have to get paper and pencil—! (*He twiddles his fingers frenziedly, and* CHARLIE *jumps to supply the need. Taking notes.*) Okay, go ahead. . . . Yep. . . . Uh-huh, I follow you. . . . Yep. . . . Sir? . . . Oh—oh, I see. . . . Yes, that's perfectly clear. . . . But wait a second! *How long* afterwards? . . . *Hello?* (*He stands holding a dead telephone, very slowly hangs up.*)

CHARLIE. (*To* THE CHIEF.) Did you have that monitored?

(THE CHIEF *nods affirmatively, but gestures for* CHARLIE *to be quiet.* STANNARD *however has not heard the question. There is a look of quiet wonderment on his face.*)

STANNARD. He sounded just like anybody. (*Then, almost with a start, he sees his wife there close beside him, staring terrified questions up into his eyes. He takes her quickly into his arms.*) It's all set now, darling—everything's going to be all right.

MRS. STANNARD. (*She instantly goes limp, so that if he were not holding her, she would fall.*) Oh, how wonderful! How good of them! (*Already deeply preoccupied with the next step,* STANNARD *beckons* DR. GORMAN *with his head, but* MRS. STANNARD *still clings.*) I'm sorry if I didn't hold up.

STANNARD. You were a miracle.

MRS. STANNARD. *I* know how I was—like a scared she-cat, all fluffed out. (*Shaking her head.*) I'm so *confused!*

(STANNARD *gently disengages himself, turns her over to* DR. GORMAN.)

STANNARD. Doctor, give this girl some sleep.

DR. GORMAN. If she just wouldn't fight my sedatives—!

MRS. STANNARD. I'll be good now—anything anybody tells me! I'll just say my prayers. (*During the following,* DR. GORMAN *half leads her toward foyer.*) Dave, I'm no good at finances. You go ahead and handle the whole thing. I'm sure nobody in the world could do it half as well. Only— (*Looking back.*) you won't let anything go wrong, will you?

STANNARD. (*Quiet.*) Nothing will go wrong.

MRS. STANNARD. (*As she exits with* GORMAN.) Oh dear, kind God the Father, I'm so scared! I'm so scared!

(*During the above,* CHARLIE *has looked keenly from speaker to speaker, like a man at a show.* STANNARD *crosses to telephone, and dials. Simultaneously* THE CHIEF *steps to bar, pours a stiff jolt.* CHARLIE *takes a fistful of peanuts.*)

THE CHIEF. Join me?

CHARLIE. (*Twistedly smiling.*) Me?—*take a drink!?*

THE CHIEF. (*Apologetic.*) Oh, yeah—I forgot.

(CHARLIE'S *eye has been caught by something on the end table. As he drifts over, casually munching peanuts—*)

STANNARD. (*On telephone.*) Al? . . . Yes, we've had contact. Listen, are you in touch with Langly? . . . Okay! I want you both here right away—and bring the books. (*Just as* STANNARD *hangs up,* CHARLIE'S *clever fingers pick up the slip of notes. Instantly* STANNARD'S *hand closes over the outstretched wrist, slowly turns it until* CHARLIE'S *fingers drop the slip of paper.* STANNARD *picks it up, pockets it, still gripping* CHARLIE'S *wrist. Neither man is angry.*) Hold off till tomorrow, 4 P. M.

CHARLIE. Exclusive?

STANNARD. (*Nodding.*) But I'll have to hold out some of the terms.

CHARLIE. (*After reflecting.*) Deal. (STANNARD *releases him, and* CHARLIE *stands rubbing his wrist, smiling sourly.*) Now we've both had an arm twisted, Mr. Stannard. (*Shrugging.*) Question is, will it get you your kid back?

THE CURTAIN COMES DOWN

END OF ACT ONE

ACT TWO

Scene 1

SCENE: *Afternoon, two days later.*

AT RISE: DR. GORMAN *is getting into his topcoat in the foyer, while a uniformed* NURSE *stands waiting to give him his hat and satchel.*

DR. GORMAN. We'll continue sedation for the present.
THE NURSE. (*Openly uneasy.*) In the same dosages?
DR. GORMAN. I think so.
THE NURSE. Doctor, if you don't mind, would—would you just write down your directions?
DR. GORMAN. Certainly. You know, Nurse, your patient's body isn't going to be a great deal of use to her without a mind to guide it. (*He writes instructions on prescription pad, gives them to her.*) Keep a close check of course.
THE NURSE. Thank you. (*Handing him hat and satchel.*) The longer I nurse for my living, the more I wonder sometimes why people want to have babies at all.
DR. GORMAN. (*Patting her hand.*) Never say that.

(*The DOORBELL rings. She goes to answer it.* AL STANNARD *enters, followed by* THE NURSE *who exits Right.* AL *is an inch or two shorter than* STANNARD, *but powerful and stocky. There is an indefinable stamp of mediocrity about him. He carries a briefcase.*)

AL. Doc—!
DR. GORMAN. Hello, Al. I was just leaving.
AL. How's the sister-in-law?
DR. GORMAN. Not much change. I'll be back later—(*An afterthought.*) By the way, your wife is doing very

nicely after her little disappointment last week. Under different circumstances, I'd say "better luck next time!"

AL. No, no, Doc! Liz and I plan to keep right on trying!

(GORMAN *exits.* AL *comes into living room as* CHARLIE *and* THE CHIEF *enter from patio.* CHARLIE *grabs a fistful of peanuts from off the bar.*)

CHARLIE. (*Pointing with peanuts.*) Who's that? (*Before* THE CHIEF *can answer.*) Oh—the brother. (*Looking* AL *over.*) Hi, Al.

AL. (*He nods coldly.*) Good afternoon, Chief.

THE CHIEF. Afternoon, Mr. Stannard.

AL. (*Crossing to secretary.*) You're here a little early, aren't you?

(CHAPMAN *enters from foyer with a tray of sandwiches and coffee, arranges this on a table, while* AL *starts laying out papers from the briefcase.*)

THE CHIEF. (*Taking sandwich.*) Good! No time for lunch today.

(*Chewing the sandwich, he crosses to front windows, and peeps out guardedly in both directions.* CHARLIE *hooks* CHAPMAN'S *arm, draws him intimately to a stop.*)

CHARLIE. Which way is the kid's bedroom? (CHAPMAN *gives him a startled glance, frees his arm, walks around* CHARLIE, *and takes up his stand at entrance.* CHARLIE *looks him over critically.*) Five bucks? (*Patient, as* CHAPMAN *still says nothing.*) Look: I just want to get a picture of his little bed with the teddy bear on it—for when our second edition comes out.

CHAPMAN. He doesn't have a teddy bear.

CHARLIE. (*Guardedly, he takes a small camera out of his pocket. Demonstrating.*) Just sight through here, and press this thing. (*Offering camera to* CHAPMAN.) *You* get the shot—same five bucks. (*As* CHAPMAN *puts his hands behind his back.*) Fifty.

CHAPMAN. (*Softly.*) Mister, you're insulting me.

CHARLIE. (*Indignant.*) *Fifty bucks is an insult!?* This is *really* inflation.

(*At this moment,* STANNARD *enters briskly from foyer.* CHAPMAN *exits.*)

STANNARD. Al! Al!

(*They meet and embrace warmly.* AL *steps back.*)

AL. (*Oddly disappointed somehow.*) Why, kid, you look better than I expected!

STANNARD. I'm fine! (*Glancing toward the secretary.*) Well, let's get on it!

AL. (*As they cross.*) Just a few signatures. To expedite, I put some of the transfers through my own account.

STANNARD. That was damn generous.

AL. Aw, stop it! What's a brother for!

(STANNARD *sits down at the secretary, and puts on a pair of spectacles, which strangely stiffen and formalize his appearance. As he signs various documents,* AL *stands at his shoulder, wielding the blotter.*)

CHARLIE. (*Hovering.*) Well, boys, the Big Edition hits the streets at 4:30—remember? (*Pointing bitten sandwich at* THE CHIEF.) And listen, Hawkshaw, none of those radio blabbers better beat us to this.

THE CHIEF. (*Irritably.*) That's all understood, Charlie! Everything's set!

(*At the secretary, the final signature is blotted,* AL *starts stowing everything back in the briefcase, and* STANNARD *removes and pockets his spectacles.*)

CHARLIE. Okay, Mr. Stannard, we've laid off for two days as per deal.

STANNARD. (*He takes the list of penciled notes out of his pocket, and puts it back without looking at it.*) The agreed price is half a million dollars.

CHARLIE. (*Whistling.*) Five hundred G's! (*Preparing to take notes.*) What denominations?

STANNARD. Old unmarked tens and twenties.

CHARLIE. That should make quite a bundle! (*Winking at* THE CHIEF.) Al here must have knocked himself out tabulating all those serial numbers in two days.

AL. (*Sighs, wags his head in sober confirmation. To* STANNARD.) I handed every last teller a $25.00 bonus. You ought to've seen their faces!

STANNARD. How soon can we be ready?

AL. (*Eyeing* CHARLIE.) We talk in front of this man?

CHARLIE. Too late to be helped, Al. My city editor has the whole story pasted in his hat right now.

(AL *waits, ignoring* CHARLIE, *until* STANNARD *nods.*)

AL. Langly ought to be here any minute.

CHARLIE. Who's this Langly character?

THE CHIEF. Their General Manager.

CHARLIE. Oh, that creep with the boys' clubs. (*To* STANNARD *again.*) What about the drop?—and delivering your kid back afterwards—

STANNARD. We aren't quite that far yet.

CHARLIE. (*Glancing up sharply from notes.*) Oh?

STANNARD. (*Staring out window.*) First we notify them that the currency is ready, and the police will hold off—then we receive further instructions.

CHARLIE. (*Doodling.*) How do you notify—run up a bed-sheet on the roof?

STANNARD. The Stannard TV program. George Portalis will wear a white dinner jacket on tonight's show.

CHARLIE. (*To* THE CHIEF.) That's a nice twist! Get it? They can watch in on any TV in this area—no chance for a stake-out. Real smart angle! (*To* STANNARD *again.*) Will Portalis be in on it?

AL. George will just take orders as usual.

CHARLIE. (*Pocketing notes.*) I bet. (*Finishing sandwich.*) Of course, Mr. Stannard, you realize it isn't strictly legal.

STANNARD. (*Blank.*) Sir?

THE CHIEF. F. C. C. ruling—no person-to-person communication over a national network.

AL. (*Exploding.*) They'd prosecute a man for trying to ransom his own son!?

THE CHIEF. Dead letter. Public opinion would never stand for enforcement.

CHARLIE. *Enforcement!?* When our paper hits the sidewalks, your brother is going to have a hundred eighty million personal friends.

STANNARD. (*Impatient.*) Let's stick to getting the boy back before morning. (CHARLIE *and* THE CHIEF *look sharply at him—then exchange a glance sidelong.* STANNARD *catches this.*) And what was that about? (*Getting no answer.*) I asked a question!

CHARLIE. (*Very reluctant.*) You—wouldn't want to be babied along on this, would you?

STANNARD. (*Dead steady.*) Let's have it, *Times-Chronicle*.

CHARLIE. (*To* THE CHIEF.) You tell him.

THE CHIEF. (*Squirming.*) Well now, Mr. Stannard, in a case of this character— I mean no man can guarantee you absolutely—that is to say—

STANNARD. (*Crashing his fist on the table.*) *Let's have it!*

CHARLIE. As of right now, your kid could be dead for two days.

STANNARD. (*He visibly goes back on his heels. Softly.*) *Dead?*

CHARLIE. (*Harsh—yet diffident.*) How does a hood figure, Mr. Stannard? If he's hot, he drops his gun in some ash can—*evidence!* Now these jokers that are holding your boy: You think they feel good about being tied down to one spot with him? So pretty soon maybe they begin telling each other that if they just had a little more elbow room— (*Breaking off bitterly.*) They aren't working for the P. T. A., you know!

(STANNARD *still stands silent, with death in his face.*)

AL. (*Exploding again.*) But that wouldn't make sense! Here they have a—a valuable piece of merchandise you might say. Now unless they're in a position to actually make delivery—
THE CHIEF. Think it over.
STANNARD. You see, Al, this—this possibility that the gentlemen have been good enough to point out—in practical effect it has no bearing at all. I'm forced to go through with the deal now on the presumption that the boy is still alive. That's the barrel they have me over: They don't need to trust *me*, but I have to trust them absolutely.
CHARLIE. (*Nodding, grim.*) That's it—trick or treat! (*As* STANNARD *turns, walks away thoughtfully. Aside to* THE CHIEF.) Get a load of this character!

(STANNARD *stands, composed and somber, walks to entrance, looks Off Right in foyer. Finally he turns, and comes back. He stands looking earnestly from* CHARLIE *to* THE CHIEF.)

STANNARD. I'm a businessman—supposed to be hardheaded. Been called shrewd. Yet here's the biggest deal I'll ever negotiate— (*A sudden catch in his voice.*) *and I don't really know the first thing about what I'm up against!* (*Humbly to* THE CHIEF.) You'll have to advise me.
THE CHIEF. (*Shying off.*) Now hold on! I just enforce the law around here.
CHARLIE. (*As* STANNARD *turns to him.*) Don't look at me, either. I just report the news like it falls. You're in there on your own, Stannard.
AL. (*Brotherly bluster.*) Not while I'm here.
CHARLIE. We'll see when the clutch comes.

STANNARD. (*He takes out his handkerchief, and wipes his face and neck.*) Maybe "advise" was too strong a word. What I want from you two is expert information—the true percentages: Now say I pay ransom to these people—

AL. Dave! We haven't time for this.

STANNARD. We'll take time. (*Still to* CHARLIE *and* THE CHIEF.) What odds the money is going to buy my son back?

CHARLIE. You really want it?

STANNARD. (*Striking the table again.*) *Yes!*

CHARLIE. (*Snapping his fingers.*) There's your odds.

STANNARD. (*Peers at him, not comprehending.*) Sorry —I'm a little tired—

THE CHIEF. On the record, it's about two-to-one you'll recover your boy whether you pay or not.

STANNARD. (*Incredulous.*) Paying ransom won't affect the outcome—*at all?*

THE CHIEF. Mr. Stannard, you can pay, and get him back; or you can pay—and not get him back.

CHARLIE. Or you can refuse payment, and lose; or you can refuse, and still get him back. (*Snapping his fingers again.*) Take your pick.

STANNARD. (*Looks wonderingly from one to the other.*) Then why do people pay?

THE CHIEF. (*A rueful chuckle.*) Lots easier for the police if they never did!

STANNARD. I don't follow that.

CHARLIE. No pay-off, no kidnap racket—that old profit motive.

STANNARD. (*His eyes widen. It is a moment before he can speak. To* THE CHIEF.) Why doesn't the Law step in!? Why don't you *prevent* people from paying!?

THE CHIEF. (*Startled.*) *Me?* How long would I hold my job in this community if I went around doing what I thought was right!?

CHARLIE. (*Wryly.*) And I saw this guy kick his way into a liquor store where two hoods were waiting with shotguns. (*To* STANNARD.) Just in case you thought that limp was flat feet.

THE CHIEF. What do you want, Charlie!—a criminal code with guts,—so I got a right to grab him for compounding a felony if he pays ransom? This is the U.S.A. for Pete's sake! We're a very humane people. Some of the biggest men in the country have made deals with kidnappers. And the voting public wouldn't stand for it any other way—even if the child is dead right from the start! (*Breaking off.*) I'm sorry for being so frank in front of you, Mr. Stannard.

(*During this,* STANNARD *remains lost in his own thoughts. Offstage, the voice of an approaching NEWSBOY has gradually become audible.*)

NEWSBOY. (*Off.*) Read all about it! Rich boy kidnapped! Get your extry paper here!

(*Simultaneously there is a squeal of BRAKES Offstage and an excited TEENAGE VOICE.*)

VOICE. (*Off.*) 309!—see? Here's the house!
CHARLIE. (*Checking wrist watch.*) We've been out for seven minutes.

(*As he switches on the TV set, two more cars arrive offstage in quick succession.* THE CHIEF *steps to front window.*)

THE CHIEF. Here's my traffic detail.
TV ANNOUNCER. (*Starting suddenly.*) —little Davie Stannard, the seven-year-old only son of D. J. Stannard, millionaire manufacturer of a well-known household appliance. Both parents are in seclusion. However there will be further bulletins as additional details—

(CHARLIE *switches it off, rejoins* THE CHIEF *and* AL *at the street window. More CARS are arriving outside now, and more VOICES.*)

THE CHIEF. (*Calling through window.*) Keep the driveway clear! Hold those people at the fence!

A COP. (*Off.*) What about these news cameras?

THE CHIEF. No pictures yet. Have the squad car call Headquarters for ten more men here.

AL. (*Shakily, looking off.*) Look at all the people!

CHARLIE. This time tomorrow, the bus lines will be running excursions. There'll be ice-cream trucks out there, and hot-dog stands, and kids to clean your windshield. You'll be able to get your pocket picked, or your picture taken. And every last soul in the crowd will be your friend—nothing in the world they wouldn't do to help. . . . But they'll tear down that picket fence for souvenirs the size of toothpicks.

AL. (*Suddenly.*) There's my car, Chief!—It's okay—they're letting him through. (*Crossing to foyer with* CHIEF—*calling.*) Chapman! You can open up the front door.

(STANNARD *has remained motionless in the mounting hubbub, changing his handkerchief absently from hand to hand as he mops his face and neck.* CHARLIE *hesitates, goes over, and puts an arm around* STANNARD'S *shoulders.*)

CHARLIE. Look, Dad, why don't you have yourself a stinkin' big drink!

STANNARD. (*Rousing slightly.*) Please help yourself, won't you?

(CHAPMAN *has been admitting someone at the front door. Now* LANGLY *lurches in through the entrance with two bulging kit-bags. He has the personality of a used-car salesman.*)

LANGLY. (*Plumping the bags down.*) Some load! (*Handing* CHIEF *a bunch of stapled sheets.*) Serial numbers. (*Spotting* STANNARD.) It's all here, Mr. Stannard. Care to check it yourself?

STANNARD. (*Disinterested.*) No.

LANGLY. As a personal favor, D.J. This has been a pretty big responsibility.

STANNARD. (*Indistinct.*) What good is it!

LANGLY. Sir?

STANNARD. The money—what good is it?

AL. (*Coming over.*) What's that you said, Dave?

STANNARD. What's the good of paying ransom!

(EVERYBODY *stares at him.* STANNARD *is not thinking about them. He looks blankly at the handkerchief, and stuffs it back in his pocket.*)

AL. But you *have* to! You *have* to pay it!

STANNARD. (*Slowly angering.*) Why? Half a million dollars *for what!?* To please the neighbors?—because it's socially acceptable?

AL. (*All at sea.*) But your boy, Dave—your son!

STANNARD. You heard! You were right here! Davie could be dead now.—And if he *is* dead, *why* is he dead? (*Jabbing his finger into* AL'*s chest.*) Because the people that have him were certain the ransom would be paid!—out of panic, and cowardice, and plain, fat-headed stupidity!

CHARLIE. He's absolutely right! Those babies don't fool with a murder rap unless they figure they're on a sure thing.

STANNARD. (*Still to* AL.) But we're assuming that Davie is still alive. *On what terms* is he still alive? *As simple insurance against their risking their necks until they know it will pay off!*

CHARLIE. And the minute Portalis walks on in that white jacket—man, you could buy the kid a hole full of quicklime with your 500 G's!

STANNARD. (*Unflinching.*) Exactly.

AL. (*Upset and confused.*) Maybe you're right, David. I'm not sure. But you have to think about protecting *yourself* a little bit.

STANNARD. (*Incredulous.*) *Myself?*

AL. How would you feel afterwards if you refused to pay and—well, something went wrong.
STANNARD. (*Wearily.*) You mean if Davie is murdered? *How will I feel after that!?* Only a childless man could ask that question.

(*Through all this,* LANGLY *has stood fidgeting. All at once he blurts into speech.*)

LANGLY. I know I'm not a member of the family, D.J.—you too, Mr. Al!—but as a long-time, loyal employee of Stannard Vacuum—
STANNARD. (*As* LANGLY *falters.*) Speak up, Lang.
LANGLY. Then what about your obligation to the stockholders? How's *the public* going to go for it!? And with our new line just hitting the display windows—!

(*For a split second,* CHARLIE *almost swings on him; even* AL *seems out-of-patience.*)

AL. Why don't you get back to the plant, Lang! We don't need you right now.
STANNARD. (*Frowning.*) No, Al—wait a minute. Maybe he has something. What *is* my public obligation in all this? Maybe that's the real issue here—maybe this is that kind of decision. . . . (*Turning it over in his mind.*) Let's look at it again: Why do we stand here now—my boy, my poor drugged wife? (*Turning to* CHARLIE *and* THE CHIEF.) You men have answered that for me. The *profit motive!* That's why my family and I have been wronged—possibly beyond hope of recovery. And not so much by these criminal morons, as by every grief-stricken parent that's been allowed to grovel before them in the past! (*He pauses, looking from face to face, earnest and appealing.*) So I ask myself: Aside from any possible consequence to my own little son, am I justified— (*Suddenly bursting out.*) in handing on this damned, insane thing to the next American family that's chosen!?
AL. (*His face has set slowly into a sullen look.*) That's just a lot of talk! You're not yourself.

STANNARD. You're my brother! Stand with me on this, Al—

AL. Not this time! I've always said that if I ever saw you heading for a real smashup— (*Breaking off—almost tender.*) Better let me take over for you, Dave boy.

STANNARD. (*Shaking his head.*) No one but myself can make this decision.

AL. You're a gambler!—a gambler's decision!

STANNARD. Yes, Al—either way I decide. . . . And that brings it down to the simple issue: Right and wrong.

AL. And what about Edith upstairs—would she go along with that?

STANNARD. At present? I suppose not.

AL. That's all I need. (*Turning to the* OTHERS.) The ransom will be paid, gentlemen! (*Back to* STANNARD.) And, Dave, if you make me pick up the tab, that'll be up to *your* conscience. But the whole country will be with *me!*

STANNARD. (*Almost gently.*) One question before you bite off more than you can chew: Suppose you *do* step into my shoes,—are you prepared to assume responsibility for your nephew's death?

AL. (*He resists desperately for a moment, then turns away with a look of defeat and shame.*) I guess you win as usual. I can't walk up to a thing like that. (*A flash of undisguised venom.*) What I'd like to know is *how YOU can!*

STANNARD. (*He stands looking at the stack of old boards in the corner.*) I happen to be the boy's father.

CURTAIN

END OF SCENE 1

ACT TWO

Scene 2

SCENE: *Early that evening. Offstage sound of the CROWD rises and falls steadily. Whenever the front door is opened for a moment, there is a white glare of police FLOODLIGHTS in the foyer.*

AT RISE: *A little swarm of TV TECHNICIANS is shoving the beautiful furnishings around as though they were studio props. A battery of lights is being assembled to bear on a small armchair. A TV camera is already set up.* GEORGE PORTALIS *and his* DRESSER *stand at the fireplace, checking George's make-up, and the fit of his new, ready-made white dinner-jacket. The two ponderous kit-bags are now open, and* AL *and* LANGLY *are carefully stacking the packages of currency on a table in front of the chair.* THE CHIEF *(now in uniform) is strategically posting a couple of* PATROLMEN, *armed with carbines. The glass doors to the garden are now closed, but outside,* SOMEONE *is knocking at them as insistent (and disregarded) as a moth. During the following, voices tend to overlap. The home TV set is being used as a monitor.*

A TECHNICIAN. (*Using viewer.*) One more light on this chair—it's a thirsty color!

SECOND TECHNICIAN. (*Yelling out front window.*) Come right in here wid it! (*He receives a heavy electric cable from outdoors, and walks it through, just as* CHAPMAN *enters from foyer followed by* CHARLIE. *To* CHAPMAN.) One side, Jack.

THE DRESSER. It's not such a bad fit, Mr. Portalis.

(PORTALIS *gives him a withering look, goes on primping.*)

DIRECTOR. (*Placing camera.*) Slide over about ten inches.

CAMERAMAN. No, Jerry! Right here I get a nice tilt over the money.

THE CHIEF. (*To the armed* PATROLMEN.) And all of it's real, boys! So keep an eye on it.

CHARLIE. Who's going to watch the boys?

THE CHIEF. *I* am!

THIRD TECHNICIAN. (*To* CHAPMAN.) Out the way, Mac.

FIRST TECHNICIAN. Hey, Jerry! What if His Nibs runs short on lines?

DIRECTOR. We cut back to the regular show at the studio.

TECHNICIAN WITH EARPHONES. Well, that's great! Because all *I* can pick up is that mob out front.

THE CHIEF. (*Going into foyer.*) I'll talk to 'em on the bull-horn.

(CHAPMAN *has spotted the moth-flutter at the garden doors, crosses, and slides back the glass panels. A diffident, balding* GENTLEMAN *stands there.*)

CHAPMAN. Can I help you, sir?

THE MAN. I'm a neighbor—live right over the hedge here.

CHAPMAN. (*A beat late.*) Mr. Digges. Yessir!

DIGGES. Terrible thing. My wife and I didn't even catch the newscast—can't get in our own driveway. Could I see Mr. Stannard?

CHAPMAN. Sorry—he's kind of rushed right now.

DIGGES. (*Watching everything, pop-eyed.*) What a terrible thing. We have to go all the way round through the Bannermans place on Maple. Yessir.

TECHNICIAN WITH EARPHONES. We're on in three minutes!

(*At the fireplace,* PORTALIS *makes a despairing gesture.*)

THE DRESSER. It's really not so bad, Mr. Portalis.

PORTALIS. It's a ho-dad outfit! Look at the lapels.

When a sponsor asks me to go before the public in a men's ready-to-wear garment, then it's time my attorneys started to hunt for the escape-hatch in my contract!

(*During the above,* STANNARD *has entered quietly from foyer. His face is gray and strained, and all but a small fraction of his attention is withdrawn now from the general hubbub, yet he has overheard* PORTALIS.)

STANNARD. A slight change of plan, George—you'll just introduce me.

PORTALIS. (*Remorseful.*) Sure—anything, boss! I keep trying to kid myself this is just another broadcast—can't face what's happened to you!

DIGGES. (*Suddenly spotting* STANNARD.) There's Stannard! If you'll just get him over here—

(*Again* STANNARD *overhears—goes over with instinctive courtesy.*)

STANNARD. You wish to see me, sir? (*Belated recognition.*) Oh—Dickson! I didn't know you without your hat.

DIGGES. Digges is the name. I—I just took the liberty to slip through the hedge—you know—the place he busted a hole in it.

STANNARD. Yes.

DIGGES. We don't have a child ourselves—guess we weren't always too nice to him. I mean sometimes he'd bother our cats—yell around here in the early morning—

STANNARD. I know.

DIGGES. (*Blurting.*) Look! If there's anything my wife and I can do for the two of you—you know—a cup of coffee—a quiet room for the Missiz to lay down in— (*Breaking off—starting again.*) I mean, look! If you're caught short for say twenny—twenny-fi' thousand, we could raise it on our home inside of two hours. What do *we* need it for!

TECHNICIAN WITH EARPHONES. Two minutes!

DIRECTOR. Okay, Mr. Stannard—we're ready!

STANNARD. (*Wringing* DIGGES' *hand.*) Thanks! I'll let you know.

DIGGES. (*As* STANNARD *turns away.*) What a terrible thing! Little skinny kid we used to yell at—!

(STANNARD *and* PORTALIS, *now changed back into his tweed jacket with* boutonniere, *converge upon the brightly lighted armchair.*)

STANNARD. Where do I sit?

FIRST CAMERAMAN. Right in the chair. Eyes about the level of my hand—don't look in the camera.

(*As* STANNARD *and* PORTALIS *take their places near the money-stacked coffee table.*)

THE CHIEF. (*Offstage, on police bull-horn.*) Your attention, folks! Attention, please, everybody! (*As CROWD babble continues.*) It is of vital importance that we have silence here for about twenty-five minutes. That can be your contribution toward the safe return of little Davie Stannard. (*As silence falls swiftly.*) Thanks, friends—that's wonderful.

(*During this,* STANNARD *has caught sight of* DR. GORMAN *peeping in at the entrance, beckons him over.*)

FIRST CAMERAMAN. Hey! The mike boom casts a shadda.

SECOND CAMERAMAN. (*Pointing at coffee table.*) Like to have this kind of dough? Invent a mike boom don't cast a shadda.

TECHNICIAN WITH EARPHONES. Sixty seconds!

STANNARD. (*As* DR. GORMAN *bends over him.*) Will she sleep through?

DR. GORMAN. I've done what I can within the limits of prudence. I've never seen anything like her resistance to tranquilizers outside of an institution— (*He regrets it at once.* STANNARD *has glanced up sharply. Squeezing*

STANNARD's *shoulder*.) Just get that boy back for her. She'll forget all this—like after childbirth. . . . If needed, I'll be having a snooze up in your guest bed room.

STANNARD. (*Detaining him.*) Doc! I hope nothing will interfere with this broadcast.

DR. GORMAN. (*Undecided and unhappy.*) Gosh, Dave —I dunno. (*Wandering Off.*) Well, I'll just drop in and have another look at her.

(*The* DIRECTOR *has been making a final check of* STANNARD *through the viewer.*)

DIRECTOR. Hey! What about make-up here!
TECHNICIAN WITH EARPHONES. Fifteen seconds!

(*Complete silence falls. A* TECHNICIAN *turns up the monitor set.*)

STATION ANNOUNCER'S VOICE. (*Recorded.*) It is now exactly 8 P. M. For the next half hour this station presents that very popular television personality, Mr. George Portalis, and his Stannard Vacuum Show.

(*A bar of the program THEME-SONG as the* DIRECTOR'S *arm sweeps down.*)

PORTALIS' VOICE. (*Recorded with a fanfare.*) Stannard *Vacuum is sweeping the Nation, friends!*

(*As the STAGE LIGHTS dim swiftly, leaving* STANNARD *and* PORTALIS *isolated in the peering glare of SPOT-LIGHTS.*)

PORTALIS. This evening, ladies and gentlemen, before going on with our usual program, there will be a short preliminary feature from the home living room of the president of our company. (*Turning to nod deferentially.*) Allow me to present Mr. D. J. Stannard.

(*As both SPOTLIGHTS concentrate on* STANNARD, *leav-*

ing PORTALIS *and the rest of the Stage in darkness,* STANNARD *lays a small, black, plain-covered book on the table with the packaged banknotes.*)

STANNARD. (*As though on TV—rather stiffly at first.*) Good evening. I suppose most of you have heard about the kidnapping of my seven-year-old son, Davie. (*Displaying a photograph.*) This is his picture. . . . His mother is unable to appear with me this evening, but we both want to thank you from our hearts for all your kind messages. (*Increasing grimness.*) However, it isn't to you good people that I now address myself. My words are directed exclusively to the man who called me here on the telephone three nights ago. At this moment, somewhere within fifty or a hundred miles, he, like yourselves, is looking at a television set, secretly waiting to hear my reply to his demands. (*Glowering into* CAMERA.) All right, then—listen: On this table you see a large sum of money —five hundred thousand dollars in United States currency, exactly as by you stipulated. All my wife and I have!—our only hope—our one defense—our single weapon. But you, Mr. Child-Stealer, sitting out there so confidently, will never come any closer to it than you are at this moment. Let me be absolutely clear about this: *No ransom will ever be paid for our son*—not a dollar! Not a penny! (*Leaning forward.*) And hear this carefully, because it's a matter of life and death to both of us: The moment my boy is harmed in any way, every last cent of this goes on your head as a reward—dead or alive! Blood money. (*Leaning back.*) Be fair to yourself. Think twice before you incur the penalty for a murder that can't possibly pay off. Instead, every detective and police officer on earth will be looking for you—every petty gangster— every corrupt, greedy woman—even your accomplices in this crime—your closest blood relations. You don't believe it? Look in the face of the person who may be listening to this broadcast with you. Then look in your own soul! What loyalty is going to hold up against half a million dollars! No! Wherever you go, in whatever rathole you may try to hide yourself, this money that you criminally coveted will track you down, and smell you out, and bring you to justice! . . . One word more: For whatever human feelings you may still have, if you'll turn the boy loose on any public thoroughfare in this nation, and later you're arrested for this or any other crime, my wife and I will bear witness that in our time of trouble, you heard a mother's appeal, and had pity on a child. (*Laying his hand upon the book on the table.*) And now—so you'll know I mean business—I swear to you, with my hand on this Testament, that while I have life and reason, I'll carry out every item of what I've just said. . . . *God hear me!*

CURTAIN

END OF ACT TWO

ACT THREE

Scene 1

SCENE: *The following morning. The street windows are shuttered now. A table is piled high with newspapers and telegrams. Offstage there is the steady, muted rumble of a large CROWD.*

AT RISE: AL, *wearing his hat and topcoat, stands glancing over the headlines.*

AL. (*Bitterly reading to himself.*) No ransom for Davie —Dad challenges kidnappers! (*He turns, as* STANNARD *enters from foyer. His face like graystone.*) Seen these headlines?

STANNARD. No.

AL. All against you but the *Times-Chronicle*. (*As he gets no answer.*) Lang's tabulating the rest of the telegrams at the plant—five-and-a-half to one thumbs down so far. (*Still no answer.*) Well, I was just leaving . . . thought of changing your mind?—if it still isn't too late, that is.

STANNARD. No.

AL. (*Crossing to foyer, carrying folded newspaper.*) Nothing I can do here, then. . . . Get out the back way —that crowd— (*Stopping, looking back.*) Does Edith know yet? (STANNARD *shakes his head. He is staring at the pile of boards in the corner.* AL's *jaws clench in exasperation. Over his shoulder.*) I'll be at the plant if you need me.

(SHIRLEY *enters in foyer from Right, carrying a breakfast tray. She and* AL *exchange a long look. After a moment,* AL *quietly lays the newspaper on the tray, and exits Left toward front door.* SHIRLEY *looks startled; then, watching* STANNARD *sidelong, she goes off Right in foyer. The DOORBELL starts ringing, and there is a loud KNOCKING at the front door.* STANNARD *seems not to hear it. In foyer* CHAPMAN *crosses to open door. The sound of the CROWD is much louder for a moment.*)

CHAPMAN'S VOICE. (*In protest.*) Please, gentlemen! Not right now! Be human—

(*A moment later* THE CHIEF *enters, followed by a lean, athletic man, in plain clothes, somewhat younger than himself. They come into living room together, very businesslike.*)

THE CHIEF. Got to see you, Mr. Stannard. This is agent Sarecki of the Federal Bureau of Investigation.

SARECKI. (*Displaying credentials.*) Afraid that broadcast of yours may have thrown in a monkey wrench. Time's of the essence now, and under the Lindbergh statute, the Bureau can't legally move in here for another four days unless you sign this release. (*Presenting paper.*) I may say that Washington strongly recommends it.

STANNARD. (*Sadly.*) Washington! (*Nevertheless he takes it, signs, and quietly hands it back to* SARECKI.)

SARECKI. (*Pocketing signed release.*) What throws us is that usually it's the ransom money leads to the criminals. In the long rung not three per cent of 'em get away with it.

STANNARD. (*Quietly bitter.*) That's of course regardless of what may or may not have happened to the victim during the interval?

SARECKI. (*Brought up short—speaking carefully.*) The Bureau doesn't operate on the level of policy. Our job is apprehending law-breakers under whatever statutes are shoved at us—and completely aside from our own personal feelings. (*He hesitates for a moment, then grabs* STANNARD'S *hand, and wrings it heartily.*) But I'd like to say good luck to you, sir! *Good luck to you!* (*Briskly turning away.*) Chief, let's get on it.

(As SARECKI *goes into foyer and exits, Left,* THE CHIEF *lingers for a moment.*)

THE CHIEF. (*Shamefaced.*) I got a message from the mayor for you: He—he feels he has to issue a statement, dissociatin' himself.

(CHAPMAN *has remained in the foyer throughout, listening. He allows the two law officers to let themselves out. Again the sound of the CROWD comes in as the front door opens. As it closes,* CHAPMAN *comes slowly into living room, his eyes on* STANNARD'S *face.*)

CHAPMAN. Let me get you a little bite of something, sir. It's been over—
STANNARD. (*In sudden anguish.*) Thirteen hours, Chapman! Not a word!—not a whisper! *What have they done to him!?*
CHAPMAN. (*His lips trembling.*) Mr. Stannard, I don't know how you hold up at all! Sometimes I can't hardly hold up my ownself! (*All at once, without apology, he rests his forehead against* STANNARD'S *shoulder, and starts to weep. Muffled and indistinct.*) That night Miz Stannard brought the little feller home from the hospital—I couldn't have been more overjoyed was it my own!
STANNARD. (*Holding him powerfully.*) Chapman! . . . Thank you, Chapman! . . . Thank you!

(*Presently* CHAPMAN *gets out a large-figured handkerchief, and carefully wipes his eyes and face. He starts to say something—but then suddenly he is staring in dread into the foyer.* EDITH STANNARD *appears in foyer from Right. Her night-dress is sweated and crumpled; her hair hangs in dank locks, and her eyes look out from the death-mask of her face, blazing yet glazed.* SHIRLEY *is at her heels, in a soundless flurry of fright.* CHAPMAN *covers his face with his hands for a moment, then slips out into foyer and* SHIRLEY *runs off after him as* EDITH STANNARD *comes unsteadily into the living room. She holds the morning paper out before her at arm's length, to confront* STANNARD *with the screaming headlines: !!NO RANSOM FOR DAVIE!! DAD KEEPS HALF MILLION.*)

MRS. STANNARD. (*Soft, thick-tongued.*) You! His own father! You did this! You!

STANNARD. (*Sick despair.*) Edith! Who let you have that!?

MRS. STANNARD. Al—bless his kind heart! Bless Al, I say! (*Unhurriedly she begins tearing the newspaper into long strips.*)

STANNARD. (*Weakly calling.*) *Nurse!*

MRS. STANNARD. She's asleep. She thought I was under again, but I fooled her. . . . Dave, why did you do this thing? Do you hate us both so much?

STANNARD. Let me take you upstairs—

MRS. STANNARD. (*In a voice which stops him.*) *Don't come near me!* I'll run to the kitchen. . . . Do you understand what I mean?

STANNARD. (*Watching her.*) Yes.

MRS. STANNARD. You fool!—to threaten them! Now they'll be raging angry—and it's Davie will pay.

STANNARD. Can you listen to me, Edith?

MRS. STANNARD. (*Sly.*) Oh, yes, I can hear you all right.

STANNARD. Then don't you remember? After the telephone contact you told me to handle everything. And whatever I've done, I still believe was—

MRS. STANNARD. Ohh—! Oh, you devil to blame me! You bribed that doctor to keep me drugged! Well, I'm the mother, and I have rights too—under the laws of life, and the United States, and before God the Father! . . . And I order you to take it back. . . .

(*The final phrase is said so casually almost, that at first* STANNARD *fails to follow.*)

STANNARD. Take what back?

MRS. STANNARD. (*An urgent whisper.*) Tell them you never meant what you said! Say you were intimidated by the newspapers or the police or something! Promise them twice the ransom they asked for—anything they want—! (*Peering at him, trying to focus.*) You won't have to eat any crow, Dave! We'll go straight to the underworld—spread money all around! Those people will get us in touch—!

STANNARD. Too late for that now.

MRS. STANNARD. How can you say such a thing? They've got him *somewhere!*

STANNARD. Darling, you don't understand—

MRS. STANNARD. Oh, but I *do,* David. (*With a sort of dinner-party malice.*) The great D. G. Stannard! Everything has to go *his* way—always has to be the big wheel whatever happens—!

STANNARD. (*Humbly patient.*) Will you try to hear me for just a minute? As soon as I finished broadcasting last night the whole thing was settled for good, one way or the other. The dice are still lying out in the dark, and there isn't a thing anybody can do until we find out how they fell.

MRS. STANNARD. But it's been hours!

STANNARD. (*Flinching.*) Fourteen. Maybe they're taking all kinds of precautions not to expose themselves returning him to us. It could still very well mean that!

MRS. STANNARD. (*She peers at him for a moment, then clasps her hands tightly, with her eyes closed.*) Oh God, make him listen to me! (*Suddenly she drops down before* STANNARD *on her knees.*) This one thing—this one thing, Dave! I'll always remember you did it for me! I'll never go against you again as long as I live. (*Trying to embrace his knees.*) Oh, please, Dave! Look at me—I'm your wife—I'm half out of my mind, and at your mercy—!

STANNARD. (*Struggling to raise her.*) Edith, I can't go through this! Get up on your feet!

MRS. STANNARD (*She remains staring up at him from her knees, then suddenly rises, and stands facing him.*

Smiling viciously.) I ought to have realized it all along: No matter what you've pretended, *you never really loved your son.* You're jealous of him.

STANNARD. (*He is silent for a moment.*) Edith, give me your hands.

MRS. STANNARD. No!

STANNARD. Give me your hands!

MRS. STANNARD. *No!* (*Yet against her will, she lets him have them.*)

STANNARD. We both love him, darling. To us, he's still as wonderful and unblemished as the day Dr. Gorman delivered him to us. . . . And that's what we're bound to act for in all this! As his parents, we're no more than trustees for what he may yet become one day, God granting! (*Hardly able to finish.*) —a man who'd never knowingly wrong his country, or his fellow men—not to save his life—

MRS. STANNARD. (*She suddenly wrenches her hands free, and screams hoarsely in his face.*) Those people out in the street—*they'll* be on my side—! (*Before* STANNARD *can guess what she is up to, she whips about, and runs into the foyer.*) Help!—Help me!

(STANNARD *follows on the run. At the same moment* CHAPMAN *and* SHIRLEY *enter from kitchen, and all three grapple* MRS. STANNARD.)

SHIRLEY. No no, honey! No no! Please now, Miz Stannard, honey. No no!

(*Now the* NURSE *comes hustling into foyer, from Right, minus her crisp cap, and gets a more professional grip on the patient.*)

THE NURSE. (*As they wrestle.*) She ought to be in restraint! She's too much to manage!

MRS. STANNARD. (*Madly, above all.*) Help!—in here! They're holding me!—it's Davie's mother! Help! Help me! Help—!

(*Then all at once the struggle is over.*)

THE NURSE. (*Panting, supporting* MRS. STANNARD.) I'll call Doctor. I can't think how she ever got herself down here—!

(STANNARD *quickly lifts his wife in his arms. Her limbs dangle as though disjointed, and her head hangs as though her neck were broken.* STANNARD *carries her out Off Left, the* NURSE *anxiously following.* CHAPMAN *and* SHIRLEY *remain looking up after them. Both are still breathless, and* SHIRLEY *is crying again.*)

CHAPMAN. This was your doing, Shirley Lorraine.
SHIRLEY. I meant right, Uncle Jesse! I meant right!

(*As she runs Off Right, sobbing,* STANNARD *comes slowly into the living room,* CHAPMAN *following.*)

CHAPMAN. You haven't so much as closed your eyes for three days! That's not intelligent, Mr. Stannard. You're the powerhouse! Who've we got without you!?

(*Swaying with exhaustion,* STANNARD *looks heavily about, sees the wing chair standing by itself, Downstage Left.*)

STANNARD. (*Crossing.*) I'll sit here a while. (*He drops into the chair, lays his head back, and closes his eyes.*)
CHAPMAN. (*Hovering.*) Likely I've mentioned it to you, sir, I'm one of the deacons at our little church, and we want you to know we're all prayin' right around the clock.

(*No answer.* CHAPMAN *realizes that* STANNARD *is already deep asleep.* CHARLIE *prowls in from the garden. Taking wads of press-releases, etc. out of various pockets, he arranges them along the bar, begins checking and annotating them with a pencil stub. He is tired and gloomy—yawns hugely, as* CHAPMAN *approaches him.*)

CHARLIE. Where's the boss?

(CHAPMAN *makes a hasty, warning gesture toward the wing chair, and the rest of the scene is played in low tones.*)

CHAPMAN. (*Wiping bar.*) How do you think it looks, Mr. Telfer?

CHARLIE. (*Scribbling notes.*) After twenty years at the keyhole, I know enough *not* to think.

CHAPMAN. Guess there's nothing left for us now but to pray. (*As* CHARLIE *does not reply.*) Care to join me, Mr. Telfer?

CHARLIE. (*He glances up startledly at him.*) I just report the news—I never attempt to influence it. (CHAPMAN *does not smile. He stands with both hands before him on the bar, a remote and inward look on his face.* CHARLIE *realizes that* CHAPMAN *is silently praying.*) You just can't believe your good Lord could pull the rug out— (*Nodding toward wing chair.*) from under this guy—huh?

CHAPMAN. *You* think He could?

CHARLIE. If *I* was the good Lord, I know *I* couldn't.

CHAPMAN. (*Peering at him.*) You're saying there's still hope!

CHARLIE. (*He raps the pencil down on the bar.*) I'm saying I'm an expert, and ever since the broadcast I've had that kidnapper in my gut! (*Clutching his own abdomen.*) Right in here crossways!

CHAPMAN. What's he up to in there?

CHARLIE. What would *you* be up to!?

CHAPMAN. *Me?*

CHARLIE. (*Vehement.*) Say *you're* holding the kid!—out on some crummy chicken ranch: So now you and your fat girl friend are getting sort of this way whether you ought to knock him off, so he doesn't jump up in court some day to put the finger on you. (*Grabbing the front of* CHAPMAN's *jacket.*) Then right away you start thinking about having this Stannard character camping on your trail with all that dough! . . . Tell me something, Jesse: Do you feel good about it?

CHAPMAN. (*A shudder.*) Not me!

CHARLIE. (*Releasing him, slapping his own stomach.*) Right! This guy in my gut is too scared to move. Can't even comb his hair, or play solitaire, or go to sleep—doesn't dare drop around to the drugstore for a pack of cigarettes. (*Striking the bar softly with his fist.*) I tell you, the two of them are worried spitless that the kid might get hit by a street car while they're trying to bring him home. . . .

(*Suddenly* CHARLIE *is listening breathlessly: The distant wail of a POLICE SIREN, swiftly approaching, and slowing down.*)

VOICES. (*Shouting Offstage.*) Clear that driveway! Get those people back out of there!

(*Forgetting* STANNARD, *asleep in the wing chair*, CHARLIE *bounds to the front window, rips it open. A rising rumble from the CROWD.*)

CHARLIE. (*Yelling Off.*) Lou! Hey, Manheim! What gives?

VOICE. (*Off, excitedly yelling back.*) They just found the crime car out on Highway 97! The kid's fingerprints are all over it!

(CHARLIE *stands stricken. Observed only by the audience,* STANNARD *has wakened in the wing chair. He sits listening for a moment, clutching the chair arms. Then he rises, and crosses slowly to Downstage Center, where he stands waiting, with his back toward the audience, facing the entrance. The front door opens and* THE CHIEF *and* SARECKI *enter foyer with an escort of* COPS, *and followed closely by a trampling rabble of* REPORTERS *and* NEWS PHOTOGRAPHERS. THE CHIEF *has a large manila envelope in his hand.*)

THE CHIEF. Where's Stannard at? Where is he!? (*They stop short at entrance as they catch sight of* STANNARD. *Silence falls, so that the rumblings of the MOB are audible again Offstage. In a strained voice, coming toward* STANNARD.) I'm afraid I have some bad news for you, Mr. Stannard. Could— (*Fumbling in the manila envelope.*) could you just identify this? We found it back of the cushions of a stolen automobile. . . .

(*As he speaks, he unfolds, and holds outspread the small white T-shirt, with the unmistakable red-white-and-blue band around the middle. But now it is soiled, and there is a dreadful, dark stain on the left side.* STANNARD *remains motionless, his shoulders stooped, his back still toward the audience. Then the whole foyer is a blinding dazzle of flash bulbs.*)

CURTAIN

END OF SCENE 1

ACT THREE

SCENE 2

SCENE: *Mid-morning the following day. The nearly drawn curtains of the street windows admit narrow slices of SUNSHINE. Offstage, the sound of the CROWD is a fluctuating mutter, with an occasional outburst of booing.*

AT RISE: STANNARD *and* LANGLY *are at the secretary, bent over a mass of documents.* STANNARD *is wearing his owlish glasses again. His voice has taken on a wooden quality. As the two conduct their business, LANGLY is covertly insolent in manner and inflection, though STANNARD appears not to notice. CHARLIE is perched on one of the stools at the bar, throwing in drink after drink, with his eyes fixed unhappily on STANNARD. THE CHIEF, in plain clothes again, stands beside him, anxious and upset.*

STANNARD. Does this issue carry a redemption penalty?
LANGLY. One point three per cent.

(CHARLIE *snaps his fingers at this paltry amount.*)

THE CHIEF. (*Hooking his arm.*) Come on, Charlie—you shouldn't be doin' this to yourself!
CHARLIE. (*Shakes him off, without removing his eyes from* STANNARD. *Half audible, half aside to* CHIEF.) Get a load of those eye-glasses—been right there since seven-eight o'clock this morning. Financial affairs. Business. See what I mean?
STANNARD. (*Signing documents.*) The accruals will make it up. Any others?
LANGLY. Right there in front of you.
STANNARD. Oh, yes—thank you.
CHARLIE. (*Muttering.*) Polite, ain't he! Whole rest of the county out siftin' the fields both sides of Highway 97—and tonight the Feds are flyin' dogs in. Ever see a flyin' dog? Really sumpm. (*Gulping another drink.*) Won't be long now, brother! That ole identification scene at City Morgue. (*Elaborate drunken sarcasm.*) 'Course we wouldn't want to interrupt any big deals around here! (LANGLY *glances over irritably toward the muttering, and* CHARLIE *reacts at once. Trying to get up.*) Shut up, you creep, you! or I'll do it for you!
THE CHIEF. For Pete's sake, Charlie! Don't make us run you in.
CHARLIE. (*Plaintive.*) Why did you remind me of cops for! Now I'll prolly slug one before I pass out.

(AL *has entered in foyer from Right. Wearing his topcoat, and carrying his hat, he looks as shaved and formal as an undertaker. He comes into the living room.*)

AL. Could you spare about half a minute? (*As* STANNARD *turns around toward him, taking his glasses off.*) Liz and I are taking Edith in with us. Gorman seems to think it's advisable for the present. It's what she wants herself—the last time she was able to talk to us, that is. (STANNARD *says nothing. He has slowly risen and now is staring into the foyer. A careful group enters foyer from Right:* DR. GORMAN *and the* NURSE, *supporting* MRS. STANNARD. *She is dressed in street clothes, but wears them as unconvincingly as a dressmaker's dummy, except that her eyes blink. As they reach living room entrance and pause,* STANNARD *comes to them. He scans his wife's face for a moment, searching it for some indication that she might still be capable of responding to him.* MRS. STANNARD *seems oblivious to his scrutiny.* AL *watches* STANNARD.) I'll take her out the back way. Any objections? (*After a moment,* STANNARD *shakes his head.* DR. GORMAN *and the* NURSE *lead* MRS. STANNARD *out past him, toward Right.* STANNARD *watches them exit.*) We decided our limousine would be better than a regular ambulance. That mob is turning ugly out there. (*As* STANNARD *makes no reply.*) I'm sincerely sorry for you, David —from every possible angle.

(*Receiving no answer, he turns, and exits, putting on his hat.* LANGLY *clears his throat.* STANNARD *comes slowly back to the secretary again, sits down, puts his glasses back on.* CHARLIE *has followed every detail with an almost agonizing attention, holding onto the bar.*)

STANNARD. (*Back to business.*) I take it this includes all my personal assets?
LANGLY. Yes.

STANNARD. In disposing of this large block, better conduct operations over a period of months. Don't want to depress the market on it.

LANGLY. Very well.

CHARLIE. (*To himself and his gods.*) Had to happen to *me*—huh? Local jerk-water Diogenes: *What a piece of work is a man.* Just a man—that's what *I* was jacklightin' for, boy!

(*His voice has risen. Now for the first time,* STANNARD *takes notice of him.*)

STANNARD. You wish something of me, sir?

CHARLIE. (*Burlesque deference.*) Oh, no no no—nobody here but jus' us peasants! Wouldn't want to louse up any of these big Stannard enterprises! (*Peering at* STANNARD *with desperate mirthlessness.*) What a piece of work is a man! Want to know sumpm, Stannard? Right up till seven-eight o'clock this morning, any time you whistled, I'd have come runnin' like a flyin' dog—retrieve your socks from under the bed—get what I mean? . . . Hadda happen to me—huh? (*Winking at* CHIEF.) Know sumpm? I know sumpm Shakespeare don't know! (*Pointing at* STANNARD.) You take all that much brains and guts, and stuff it into one guy, and there ain't any room left for a heart! (*Suddenly rising, looking around blindly.*) Hey, get me out of here, will you—I gotta be sick. (THE CHIEF *grabs his arm, and they head for the garden with a sense of emergency. As they exit.*) Shouldn't happen to a flyin' dog—huh?

(STANNARD *blinks after them, already forgetting that they have ever been in the room. The sound of the CROWD rises and falls Offstage.*)

STANNARD. (*Arranging papers.*) Everything is quite clear?

LANGLY. Completely, D.J.

STANNARD. (*Leaning back, eyes remote.*) What I have

in mind is a sort of permanent foundation—one that will keep operating without personal supervision—with no dependence at all on my continued activity—

LANGLY. (*Visibly brightening.*) Oh? Then Mr. Al will be giving orders at the Plant?

STANNARD. Yes. . . . Now of course, if by the end of say twenty years, the murderers of my son still haven't been brought to justice, then this entire new fund—

LANGLY. (*Impatiently and disrespectfully completing the phrase.*) —will be applied to the next case of a similar nature! (*A half brick crashes through one of the street windows, rolls to a stop under the spinet. There is a shrilling of POLICE WHISTLES Offstage.* STANNARD *has glanced over absently, but* LANGLY *jumps up in apprehension. Nervously stuffing papers into briefcase.*) We'll get on it first thing tomorrow morning, D.J.

STANNARD. Get on it today.

LANGLY. Very well. (*Hardly noticed,* CHAPMAN *appears in the foyer, peeps in, spots the broken glass, etc., disappears again.* LANGLY *zips up the briefcase.*) I've already spoken to the I. R. man—he feels that as long as the funds are derived from dividends, they'll probably be tax free.

STANNARD. Good.

LANGLY. (*Watching him sidelong.*) The ransom payment would probably have been deductible, too. (STANNARD *makes no answer. He takes off his glasses, and remains seated, his hands lying idle on the secretary.*) Well, good-bye, then, D.J.

STANNARD. Good-bye.

(*With a final nervous glance toward the street window,* LANGLY *walks away briskly. But in the foyer, he cannot quite let it go.*)

LANGLY. (*Halting—looking back.*) At least you have the comfort of knowing you did what you felt was right.

(STANNARD *does not reply or move. As* LANGLY *exits through foyer, toward Right,* STANNARD *stands up slowly, closes and locks the secretary, and drops the key into his pocket.*)

STANNARD. (*Softly to himself.*) Right—! (CHAPMAN *reappears with a dustpan and brush, comes into the room, kneels, and sweeps up the broken glass.* STANNARD *is looking across at the boards which still stand in the corner. He crosses slowly, his eyes fixed on them, and stops a few feet off. Carrying the loaded dustpan,* CHAPMAN *goes from one street window to the next, drawing the curtains close shut against the DAYLIGHT. Suddenly* STANNARD *breaks into great, tearless sobs. He collapses to his knees, hugging the boards, thrusting his face against them.*) Right! . . . Right! . . .

(CHAPMAN *sets the dustpan down, crosses swiftly, and bends over* STANNARD, *embracing his heaving shoulders until the sobs begin to subside.*)

CHAPMAN. (*His own voice breaking.*) And King David was much moved, and thus he said, O my son Absalom! my son, my son Absalom! would God I had died for thee, O Absalom, my son, my son!

(*As* CHAPMAN *straightens,* STANNARD *is quiet, though he remains bowed, with his forehead against the boards.* CHAPMAN *softly draws the curtains across the open garden doors, retrieves the loaded dustpan, and turns off the LIGHT in the bar. He crosses to entrance, looks back toward* STANNARD, *goes into foyer, exits Right. After several moments, the curtains across the garden doors seem to be disturbed by a breath of air. Then* DAVIE *stands there in the dimness, looking down at his* FATHER *in surprise.*)

DAVIE. (*Softly.*) Daddy! (STANNARD *scrambles half to his feet, harkening wild-eyed. Touching* STANNARD'S *shoulder.*) Dad. (*Still in terror that it may be some illusion,* STANNARD *turns slowly, and sees* DAVIE, *his hair neatly brushed, and now wearing a brand new T-shirt, fancifully decorated with comic strip characters. For a moment* STANNARD *cannot speak or move—then, with a gasp, he catches the boy in his arms.* DAVIE *is somewhat embarrassed by so much emotion.*) Who are all those people? They wouldn't even let me through the front door.

(STANNARD *holds him at arm's length, struggling not to frighten the boy with his own insupportable joy.*)

STANNARD. Where did you get that awful-looking shirt?
DAVIE. (*Proud of shirt.*) He gave it to me—said I was to be careful not to come down with pumonia on him.
STANNARD. But your own shirt had blood on it!
DAVIE. (*Definitely guilty.*) Well, you see, that fat nurse-lady you sent to school after me—well, I finally had to bite her thumb a little bit, and she bleeded. . . . You need a shave, Dad.
STANNARD. (*Rising, taking* DAVIE'S *hand.*) Come on, Davie—your mother wants you.
DAVIE. (*Hanging back.*) But those people out front! They were wrecking our fence down.
STANNARD. They're all your friends, really—I think they'll be glad to see you.
DAVIE. (*Suddenly spotting the boards.*) Gai! You remembered my planks! I bet we get to finish our fort now all right!
STANNARD. Yes, son! *Yes!*

(*Rather apologetically he knuckles his cheeks dry, leads* DAVIE *out into the foyer, and exits Left with him.* CHAPMAN, *looking after them, appears in foyer from Right. As a huge bellow of recognition is torn out of the Offstage CROWD,* CHAPMAN *stretches his arms wide, looking radiantly upward.*)

CHAPMAN. (*The old revival shout.*) This my son was dead, and is alive again! He was lost, and is found!

END OF ACT THREE

FINAL CURTAIN

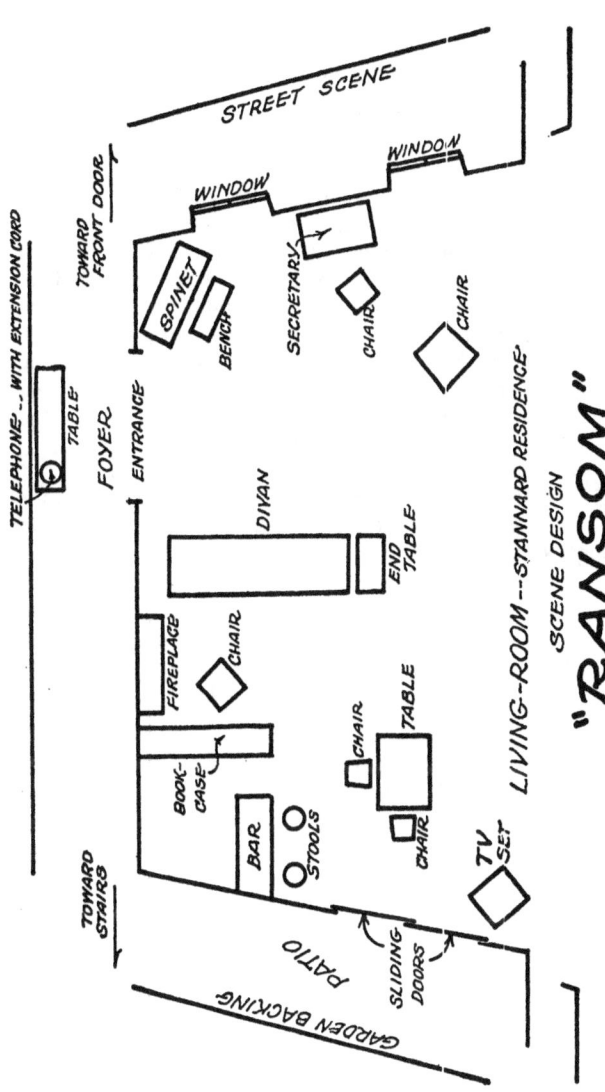

WHITE BUFFALO
Don Zolidis

Drama / 3m, 2f (plus chorus)/ Unit Set

Based on actual events, WHITE BUFFALO tells the story of the miracle birth of a white buffalo calf on a small farm in southern Wisconsin. When Carol Gelling discovers that one of the buffalo on her farm is born white in color, she thinks nothing more of it than a curiosity. Soon, however, she learns that this is the fulfillment of an ancient prophecy believed by the Sioux to bring peace on earth and unity to all mankind. Her little farm is quickly overwhelmed with religious pilgrims, bringing her into contact with a culture and faith that is wholly unfamiliar to her. When a mysterious businessman offers to buy the calf for two million dollars, Carol is thrown into doubt about whether to profit from the religious beliefs of others or to keep true to a spirituality she knows nothing about.

TREASURE ISLAND
Ken Ludwig

All Groups / Adventure / 10m, 1f (doubling) / Areas
Based on the masterful adventure novel by Robert Louis Stevenson, *Treasure Island* is a stunning yarn of piracy on the tropical seas. It begins at an inn on the Devon coast of England in 1775 and quickly becomes an unforgettable tale of treachery and mayhem featuring a host of legendary swashbucklers including the dangerous Billy Bones (played unforgettably in the movies by Lionel Barrymore), the sinister two-timing Israel Hands, the brassy woman pirate Anne Bonney, and the hideous form of evil incarnate, Blind Pew. At the center of it all are Jim Hawkins, a 14-year-old boy who longs for adventure, and the infamous Long John Silver, who is a complex study of good and evil, perhaps the most famous hero-villain of all time. Silver is an unscrupulous buccaneer-rogue whose greedy quest for gold, coupled with his affection for Jim, cannot help but win the heart of every soul who has ever longed for romance, treasure and adventure.

SAMUELFRENCH.COM

www.ingramcontent.com/pod-product-compliance
Lightning Source LLC
Chambersburg PA
CBHW070648300426
44111CB00013B/2322